D1172826

At Issue

Should There Be an International Climate Treaty?

Other Books in the At Issue Series:

At Issue

Should There Be an International Climate Treaty?

Susan Hunnicut, Book Editor

GREENHAVEN PRESS
A part of Gale, Cengage Learning

Detroit • New York • San Francisco • New Haven, Conn • Waterville, Maine • London

Christine Nasso, *Publisher*
Elizabeth Des Chenes, *Managing Editor*

© 2011 Greenhaven Press, a part of Gale, Cengage Learning.

Gale and Greenhaven Press are registered trademarks used herein under license.

For more information, contact:
Greenhaven Press
27500 Drake Rd.
Farmington Hills, MI 48331-3535
Or you can visit our Internet site at gale.cengage.com

For product information and technology assistance, contact us at

Gale Customer Support, 1-800-877-4253
For permission to use material from this text or product, submit all requests online at www.cengage.com/permissions

Further permissions questions can be emailed to permissionrequest@cengage.com

Articles in Greenhaven Press anthologies are often edited for length to meet page requirements. In addition, original titles of these works are changed to clearly present the main thesis and to explicitly indicate the author's opinion. Every effort is made to ensure that Greenhaven Press accurately reflects the original intent of the authors. Every effort has been made to trace the owners of copyrighted material.

Cover Image copyright © Images.com/Corbis.

LIBRARY OF CONGRESS CATALOGING-IN-PUBLICATION DATA

Should there be an international climate treaty? / Susan Hunnicut, book editor.
    p. cm. -- (At issue)
Includes bibliographical references and index.
ISBN 978-0-7377-5169-7 (hardcover) -- ISBN 978-0-7377-5170-3 (pbk.)
1. Greenhouse gas mitigation--Government policy--United States. 2. Climatic changes--Prevention--Government policy--United States. 3. Environmental policy--International cooperation. 4. Treaties. I. Hunnicut, Susan. II. Title. III. Series.
    TD885.5.G73S55 2011
    363.738'745610973--dc22
                                                                    2010053902

Printed in the United States of America
1 2 3 4 5 6 7 15 14 13 12 11

Contents

Introduction

In the weeks leading up to the 2009 United Nations Climate Change Conference, held in Copenhagen, Denmark, politicians, economists, scientists, and activists from around the world shared the belief that a binding international agreement to reduce emissions of CO_2 (carbon dioxide) and other heat-trapping gases was not only necessary but urgently needed. "If we take no action to stabilize the concentration of greenhouse gases in the atmosphere, then average temperature by the end of this century would increase anywhere from 1.1 degrees to 6.4 degrees C [Celsius]," stated Rajendra Pachauri, chairman of the Intergovernmental Panel on Climate Change. Citing widely accepted, peer-reviewed scientific research, Pachauri predicted that increases in the earth's average temperature would lead to drastic climactic changes: the disappearance of sea ice by the end of the twenty-first century, increased frequency of extreme hot and cold temperatures, heavy precipitation and tropical storm intensity, decreased water resources in semi-arid regions, and the possibility of widespread species extinctions. In all, 192 nations chose to be represented at Copenhagen, giving credence to the general perception that the time for decisive action had arrived. "We can go into extra time," one British diplomat noted, "but we can't afford a replay."

Yet, in spite of widespread support for a climate treaty or accord, few believed an agreement would be achieved. Negotiators remained deeply divided over two key issues, emissions targets and the level of financial assistance that should be provided by developed nations to mitigate the cost of compliance by poorer nations that have not contributed as much to global warming. It was generally believed unlikely that the conference could succeed in drafting a document that would win the approval of the US Senate, a key element of any truly meaningful international climate treaty.

In late November 2009, days before the conference was to begin, hackers broke into a server at the University of East Anglia, a respected climate research center in England, and stole thousands of e-mails and other documents which they claimed proved that climate scientists have manipulated data to overstate the case for global warming. The e-mail messages, written by English and American researchers, covered a thirteen-year period. They included detailed discussions about data that was not always easy to interpret, and whether it should be released; conversations about how best to refute the arguments of climate change skeptics; and unflattering comments about individuals known for their critical stances on the science of global warming. The most damaging e-mail, by a prominent East Anglia researcher, described a "trick" he used to "hide the decline" in a multi-century chart that purported to illustrate a global warming trend in recent years. While he later insisted that he had used the word trick with reference to a statistical technique, the need to "hide the decline" was much more difficult—though perhaps not impossible—to explain. Once the documents were posted on the Internet, climate change skeptics zeroed in on that language, launching an all-out campaign to discredit the science of anthropogenic global warming. "This is not a smoking gun; this is a mushroom cloud," concluded one scientist who has long questioned the theory that climate change is driven by human activity.

In the wake of the document theft, the University of East Anglia defended the work of its researchers. The arguments of climate skeptics were dismissed, citing a "strong consensus view" that human activity is causing harmful changes to the world's climate. "The selective publication of some stolen e-mails and other papers taken out of context is mischievous and cannot be considered a genuine attempt to engage with this issue in a responsible way," the university said in a statement. An article published in the *New York Times* a few days later concurred: "The evidence pointing to a growing human contribution to global warming is so widely accepted that the hacked material is unlikely to erode the overall argument," the article stated. "However, the documents will undoubtedly raise questions about the quality of research on some specific questions and the actions of some scientists." On December 8, fifty-six newspapers in forty-five countries weighed in, publishing a joint editorial, "Fourteen Days to Seal History's Judgment on this Generation." "The science is complex but the facts are clear," the editorial stated. "The world needs to take steps to limit temperature rises to 2° C, an aim that will require global emissions to peak and begin falling within the next 5–10 years. . . . The controversy over e-mails by British researchers that suggest they tried to suppress inconvenient data has muddied the waters but failed to dent the mass of evidence on which these predictions are based."

In the end, the outcome of the Copenhagen Climate Change Conference, though widely viewed as disappointing by those most committed to a binding international treaty to reduce greenhouse gas emissions, was probably not significantly different as a result of the release of the East Anglia documents. Negotiators were already seriously challenged by the issues of emissions targets and aid to developing nations. But in the midst of negotiations, questions about the science of global warming only complicated the discussion. The question raised by those documents—about the reliability of the science supporting the claim that climate change is caused by human actions—is one of many issues explored in *At Issue: Should There Be an International Climate Treaty?*

1

A Brief History of International Climate Negotiations

Setsuko Kamiya

Setsuko Kamiya is a staff writer for The Japan Times.

Global warming has attracted a great deal of international attention. Despite universal agreement on the need to combat climate change, it has proven difficult to craft an international treaty that all sides, and especially the United States, will agree to. Strong political commitment of all parties will be required both to achieve an agreement and to move toward its implementation.

Industrialization in the 19th century brought many of the benefits we enjoy in the modern world, changing the structure of society, industry and economy. But nearly two centuries later, one of the downsides of the Industrial Revolution is gaining more attention: global warming.

Not a day goes by without headlines on the threat posed by greenhouse gas emissions—a new report on the consequences of global warning, updates on the prospects for the United Nations COP15 [the fifteenth Conference of Parties] conference on climate change from Dec. 7 to 18 [2009].

A History of Difficulties

A closer look at the history of the biggest-ever international conference on climate change shows just how difficult a task it will be for U.N. [United Nations] member states to sign a binding agreement to curb greenhouse gas emissions, despite universal agreement on the need to fight global warming.

A preliminary meeting on the COP (conference of parties) was held in Rio de Janeiro, Brazil, at the Earth Summit in June 1992.

At that meeting, 154 countries signed the Framework Convention on Climate Change (FCCC), a treaty that committed signatories to voluntary cuts in greenhouse gas emissions, with the goal of bringing those emissions down to 1990 levels by the year 2000.

The convention recognized the global climate system as a shared resource whose stability can be affected by carbon dioxide and other greenhouse gases. But since developed countries were the main emitters of greenhouse gases, much of the convention was devoted to recommendations for those countries, objectives that they should set, and commitments that they should fulfill.

The convention entered into force March 21, 1994, after ratification by more than 50 countries in December 1993. To date, 192 countries have ratified the convention, according to the FCCC. The first meeting of the signatories, COP1, took place in Berlin [Germany] in 1995.

At the end of the meeting, a U.N. ministerial declaration known as the "Berlin Mandate" was issued, committing the parties to a comprehensive menu of actions they could select from to tackle climate change, depending on their needs.

At the COP2, in Geneva [Switzerland] in 1996, it was agreed that the protocol under negotiation on climate change would commit the parties to achieving the goals laid out in the earlier meetings.

An Important First Step

It was not until COP3 in Kyoto [Japan] in 1997, five years after the preliminary meeting in Rio, that industrialized nations finally agreed to numerical targets for cuts in carbon dioxide emissions.

The Kyoto Protocol "marks a first major international step in preventing further global warming from occurring," said Prime Minister [of Japan] Ryutaro Hashimoto, who hosted the meeting.

The Kyoto Protocol committed major greenhouse gas emitters to an average reduction of 5 percent compared with 1990 levels between 2008 and 2012, with the European Union [EU] agreeing to an 8 percent reduction, the United States to a 7 percent cut and Japan to a cut of 6 percent.

After an all-night negotiation, the parties adopted the Kyoto Protocol on Dec. 11, [1997] setting legally binding targets for cutting greenhouse gases for 37 industrialized countries and the EU.

The protocol, recognizing that developed countries, through their industrial activities, are primarily responsible for the high level of greenhouse gas emissions, imposes a heavier responsibility on them for reductions. It commits all parties to stabilizing their emissions under the principle of "common but differentiated responsibilities."

The protocol obliges signatories to meet their targets primarily through national efforts. But it allows for the flexible use of market-based mechanisms to meet the targets in the most cost-effective manner, through emissions trading, joint implementation of projects and the Clean Development Mechanism, which allows developed countries to count emissions reductions projects in developing countries against their own emissions.

Despite Hashimoto's boast, the road to implementation of the Kyoto Protocol has been rocky.

Negotiations on a "Plan of Action" to achieve the goals set forth in the protocol, which were supposed to be wrapped up by 2000, broke down at the COP6 meeting in The Hague [Netherlands].

Nations were deadlocked on several key issues, including details on an international emissions trading system, financial assistance to developing countries and the rules for counting emission reductions from "carbon sinks" such as forests.

An agreement was finally hammered out in the Bonn Agreement of 2001 [in Germany]. It covered rules for the market-based mechanisms established under the protocol, funding of developing countries' climate change efforts, crediting of carbon dioxide absorption by forests and other sinks, and the compliance mechanism for the Kyoto Protocol targets.

[In March 2001] U.S. President George W. Bush was quoted as saying . . . "We also have an energy crisis. And the idea of placing caps on carbon dioxide does not make economic sense for America."

In 2001, the US Walked Away

But the effectiveness of the still-young treaty was thrown into doubt by the world's biggest greenhouse gas emitter at the time, the U.S., walking away from the international framework in March 2001.

"Our economy has slowed down in our country," U.S. President George W. Bush was quoted as saying. "We also have an energy crisis. And the idea of placing caps on carbon dioxide does not make economic sense for America."

Without U.S. participation, the American delegation was relegated to observer status, as negotiations moved forward.

Meanwhile, with Russia, the third-largest emitter, ratifying the treaty in 2004, the minimum of 55 countries accounting for at least 55 percent of global emissions had signed on, bringing the Kyoto Protocol into force. That year also marked the 10th anniversary of the FCCC and COP10 in Buenos Aires, Argentina, celebrated the occasion.

On Feb. 16, 2005, 90 days after Russia's ratification, the Kyoto Protocol took full effect. As of November this year, 185 parties to the convention have ratified the agreement, according to the FCCC.

COP11 was held in Montreal [Canada] between November and December 2005. It marked the first time a successor to the Kyoto Protocol, which expires in 2013, was discussed.

Given the meager results of the Kyoto Protocol in terms of actual emissions cuts, a new framework extending beyond 2013 was seen as the best way of dispelling the gloom and restoring momentum to the fight against climate change. That is what countries have been doing in the past several years.

The Bali Action Plan

In 2007, the international community took a decisive step in Bali, Indonesia, in their discussion for a "post-Kyoto" treaty. Parties at the COP13 negotiations adopted the "Bali Action Plan," which committed them to a follow-up agreement to the Kyoto Protocol by the time of COP15 in Copenhagen, Denmark, in December 2009.

New governments have taken office around the world, including the administrations of U.S. President Barack Obama and Prime Minister [of Japan] Yukio Hatoyama, both of whom have taken a more proactive stance on climate change than their predecessors. That has raised hopes for an effective political agreement to be reached in Copenhagen.

Whether rising industrial powers such as China and India, which have become major greenhouse gas emitters are willing to assume some of the burden of cutting emissions will also be critical to the success of a post-2013 framework.

Strong political commitment is necessary not only for a post-Kyoto Protocol agreement but also to create a road map for its implementation process.

2

Science Predicts the Risk of Climate Change

Rajendra K. Pachauri

Rajendra K. Pachauri is chair of the Intergovernmental Panel on Climate Change (IPCC). He is also director general of The Energy and Resources Institute (TERI), an Indian research and policy organization, and director of the Yale Climate and Energy Institute.

The IPCC's Fourth Assessment Report has been approved by all the governments of the world. The report documents worldwide increases in average temperatures and predicts future increases through the end of the 21st century. These increases are likely due to increases in greenhouse gas concentrations resulting from human activity. Without worldwide action to control emissions of greenhouse gases, a number of adverse consequences—including disappearance of sea ice, frequency of hot extremes and heavy precipitation, and widespread extinctions—are likely to result. The international community has a responsibility to act to avert these developments.

Excellencies, members of the media, distinguished ladies and gentlemen! I speak to you in the voice of the world's scientific community, which in November 2007 completed IPCC's [Intergovernmental Panel on Climate Change] Fourth Assessment Report (AR4), the collective effort of almost four thousand of the world's best specialists working tirelessly over five years. The uniqueness of this mammoth exercise lies in

Rajendra K. Pachauri, speech before the UN General Assembly, September 22, 2009. Reproduced by permission.

the fact that all the governments of the world—your own governments—approved of this report, and therefore have full ownership of its contents, some salient features of which I mention now.

We stated, "Warming of the climate system is unequivocal as is now evident from observations of increases in global average air and ocean temperatures, widespread melting of snow and ice and rising global sea level", and that "Most of the observed increase in temperatures since the mid-20th century is very likely due to the observed increase in anthropogenic [caused by humans] GHG [greenhouse gas] concentrations". In the twentieth century average global temperature increased by 0.740 C [Celsius] while sea level rise resulting from thermal expansion of the ocean and melting of ice across the globe amounted to 17 cms. With this increase the Maldive Islands with land surface barely a metre or two above sea level, every storm surge and major upwelling of the seas represents a major danger to life and property. But this is not all. Climate change is already resulting in an increase in the frequency, intensity and duration of floods, droughts and heat waves. Precipitation has increased significantly in eastern parts of North and South America, northern Europe and northern and central Asia, whereas it declined in the Sahel, the Mediterranean, southern Africa and parts of south Asia. Globally the area affected by drought has increased since the 1970s. The frequency of heavy precipitation events (or proportion of total rainfall from heavy falls) has increased over most areas.

An Unacceptable Trend

If we take no action to stabilize the concentration of greenhouse gases in the atmosphere, then average temperature by the end of this century would increase anywhere from 1.1 degrees to 6.4 degrees C. The world is increasing its emissions at a rate that may take us to the upper end of the range projected, which implies a total increase in these two centuries of over 7 degrees C, that is, over 12 degrees Fahrenheit. Yet between 1970 and 2004 global GHG emissions increased by 70% and carbon dioxide by 80%. We must halt this unacceptable trend.

Climate change, in the absence of mitigation policies would in all likelihood lead to:

1. Possible disappearance of sea ice by the latter part of the 21st century

2. Increase in frequency of hot extremes, heat waves and heavy precipitation

3. Increase in tropical cyclone intensity

4. Decrease in water resources due to climate change in many semi-arid areas, such as the Mediterranean Basin, western United States, southern Africa and north-eastern Brazil

5. Possible elimination of the Greenland ice sheet and a resulting contribution to sea level rise of about 7 metres [m]—Without mitigation future temperatures in Greenland would compare with levels estimated for 125,000 years ago when palaeoclimate information suggests 4 to 6 m of sea level rise.

6. Approximately 20 to 30% of species assessed so far are likely to be at increased risk of extinction if increases in global average warming exceed 1.5 to 2.5 degrees C.

In Africa, by 2020, between 75 and 250 million people are projected to be exposed to water stress due to climate change, and in some countries yields from rainfed agriculture could be reduced by up to 50%. The impacts of climate change would be disproportionately severe on some of the poorest regions and communities of the world. My own analysis suggests that at least 12 countries are likely to tend towards becoming failed states and communities and several other states would show potential for serious conflict due to scarcity of food, water stress and soil degradation.

Beneficial Actions Will Not Be Costly

Mitigation of emissions is essential, and the IPCC has assessed its costs as modest. To limit average temperature increase at 2.0 and 2.4 degrees C, the cost of mitigation by 2030 would not exceed 3% of the global GDP [gross domestic product]. In other words, the so-called prosperity expected in 2030 would be postponed by just a few months. Further, mitigation carries many co-benefits, such as lower levels of air pollution and associated health benefits, higher energy security, larger employment and stable agricultural production, ensuring greater food security. A portfolio of technologies, currently available or expected to be commercialized, enable stringent mitigation efforts being mounted today.

Avoiding the impacts of climate change through mitigation of emissions would provide incalculable benefits including economic expansion and employment.

It is heartening that the G8 [group of leading industrialized nations] leaders have recognized the broad scientific view of limiting increase in global average temperature to 2° C. But, we have clearly specified that if temperature increase is to be limited to between 2.0 and 2.4° C, global emissions must peak no later than 2015. That is only six years from now. And the 2.0° ceiling too would lead to sea-level rise on account of thermal expansion alone of 0.4 to 1.4 meters. This increase added to the effect melting of snow and ice across the globe, could submerge several small island states and Bangladesh.

Avoiding the impacts of climate change through mitigation of emissions would provide incalculable benefits including economic expansion and employment. If those in this August gathering do not act on time, all of us would become leaders and citizens of failed states, because we would be failing in our sacred duty to protect this planet, which gives life to all species. Science leaves us with no space for inaction now.

3

The Case for Climate Change Is Based on Fraudulent Science

Paul Joseph Watson

Paul Joseph Watson is a frequent contributor to PrisonPlanet .com.

E-mail messages located on servers of the Climatic Research Unit in East Anglia that were leaked to the media in late 2009 provide conclusive evidence of fraud on the part of climate researchers attempting to document evidence of anthropocentric global warming. The e-mail messages reveal that scientists artificially adjusted data that did not support theories of climate change, that they actively sought to discredit researchers who did not agree with their conclusions, and that they interfered with requests for their data made under the Freedom of Information Act.

Calls for an independent inquiry into what is being dubbed "Climategate" are growing as the foundation for manmade global warming implodes following the release of emails which prove researchers colluded to manipulate data in order to "hide the decline" in global temperatures.

Former British chancellor Lord [Nigel] Lawson was the latest to demand an impartial investigation be launched into the scandal, which arrives just weeks before the UN [United

Nations] climate conference in Copenhagen [Denmark, in December 2009]. "They should set up a public inquiry under someone who is totally respected and get to the truth," he told the BBC Radio Four Today programme.

The emails were leaked . . . after hackers penetrated the servers of the Climatic Research Unit [CRU], which is based at the University of East Anglia, in eastern England. The CRU is described as one of the leading climate research bodies in the world.

A Conspiracy to Falsify Data

The hacked documents and communications reveal how top scientists conspired to falsify data in the face of declining global temperatures in order to prop up the premise that manmade factors are driving climate change. Others illustrate how they embarked on a venomous and coordinated campaign to ostracize climate skeptics and use their influence to keep dissenting reports from appearing in peer-reviewed journals, as well as using cronyism to avoid compliance with Freedom of Information Act requests.

As expected, the establishment media has gone into whitewash overdrive, characterizing the emails as evidence of "rancor" amongst the climate community and focusing on some of the lesser emails while ignoring the true significance of what has been revealed.

Data that has been "artificially adjusted to look closer to the real temperatures" is false data, yielding a false result.

Organizations with close ties to the CRU have engaged in psychological terrorism by fearmongering about the planet with doomsday scenarios, illustrating their argument with outlandish propaganda animation videos which show pets drowning and others that show computer-generated polar bears crashing to earth in a throwback to 9/11 [2001 terrorist attacks] victims jumping from the towers, when in reality polar bear population figures are thriving.

One of the emails under scrutiny, written by Phil Jones, the centre's director, in 1999, reads: "I've just completed Mike's Nature [the science journal] trick of adding in the real temps to each series for the last 20 years (ie, from 1981 onwards) and from 1961 for Keith's to *hide the decline*," reports the *London Telegraph*.

The author admitted to the Associated Press that the email was genuine.

In another example, researchers discuss data that is "artificially adjusted to look closer to the real temperatures". Apparently, the "real temperatures" are whatever global warming cheerleaders want them to be.

As Anthony Watts writes, attempts to claim emails are "out of context," as the defense has been from CRU, cannot apply in this instance.

You can claim an email you wrote years ago isn't accurate saying it was "taken out of context", but a programmer making notes in the code does so so that he/she can document what the code is actually doing at that stage, so that anyone who looks at it later can figure out why this function doesn't plot past 1960. In this case, it is not allowing all of the temperature data to be plotted. Growing season data (summer months when the new tree rings are formed) past 1960 is thrown out because "these will be artificially adjusted to look closer to the real temperatures", which implies some post processing routine.

Spin that, spin it to the moon if you want. I'll believe programmer notes over the word of somebody who stands to gain from suggesting there's nothing "untowards" about it.

Either the data tells the story of nature or it does not. Data that has been "artificially adjusted to look closer to the real temperatures" is false data, yielding a false result.

The Cardinal Sin of Scientific Research

Another email discusses changing temperature data to fix "blips" in studies so as to make them conform with expectations, which of course is the cardinal sin of scientific research.

"Conspiracy, collusion in exaggerating warming data, possibly illegal destruction of embarrassing information, organized resistance to disclosure, manipulation of data, private admissions of flaws in their public claims and much more" was revealed in the 61 megabites of confidential files released on the Internet for anyone to read, writes Andrew Bolt.

Another email appears to celebrate the death of climate change skeptic John L Daly, with the words, "In an odd way this is cheering news."

In another communication, the author expresses his fantasy to "beat the crap out of" climate change skeptics.

In another exchange, researchers appear to discuss ways to discredit James Saiers of the *Geophysical Research Letters* journal, by means of an academic witch hunt, because of his sympathies with climate change skeptics.

"If you think that Saiers is in the greenhouse skeptics camp, then, if we can find documentary evidence of this, we could go through official AGU [American Geophysical Union] channels to get him ousted."

Other emails express doubt about whether the world is really heating up and infer that data needs to be reinterpreted.

"The fact is that we can't account for the lack of warming at the moment and it is a travesty that we can't. The CERES [Clouds and Earth's Radiant Energy System] data published in the August *BAMS* 09 supplement [*Bulletin of the American Meteorological Society*] on 2008 shows there should be even more warming: but the data are surely wrong. Our observing system is inadequate."

Scientists discuss trying to disguise historical data that contradicts the man-made climate change thesis, such as the Medieval Warm Period (MWP), which must be 'contained' according to one email.

Suppression of evidence is also discussed, with scientists resolving to delete embarrassing emails.

Dismissing Those Who Disagree

"And, perhaps most reprehensibly," writes James Delingpole, "a long series of communications discussing how best to squeeze dissenting scientists out of the peer review process. How, in other words, to create a scientific climate in which anyone who disagrees with AGW [anthropogenic global warming] can be written off as a crank, whose views do not have a scrap of authority."

"This was the danger of always criticising the skeptics for not publishing in the 'peer-reviewed literature'. Obviously, they found a solution to that—take over a journal! So what do we do about this? I think we have to stop considering 'Climate Research' as a legitimate peer-reviewed journal. Perhaps we should encourage our colleagues in the climate research community to no longer submit to, or cite papers in, this journal. We would also need to consider what we tell or request of our more reasonable colleagues who currently sit on the editorial board. . . . What do others think?"

"I will be emailing the journal to tell them I'm having nothing more to do with it until they rid themselves of this troublesome editor." "It results from this journal having a number of editors. The responsible one for this is a well-known skeptic in NZ [New Zealand]. He has let a few papers through by Michaels and Gray in the past. I've had words with Hans von Storch about this, but got nowhere. Another thing to discuss in Nice!"

Scientists also "discussed ways of dodging Freedom of Information Act requests to release temperature data," reports the *Daily Mail.*

The emails show that scientists relied on cronyism and cosying up to FOIA [Freedom of Information Act] officials to prevent them from being forced to release data.

When the FOI [Freedom of Information] requests began here, the FOI person said we had to abide by the requests,' the email says. "It took a couple of half-hour sessions to convince them otherwise."

"Once they became aware of the types of people we were dealing with, everyone at UEA [University of East Anglia] became very supportive. I've got to know the FOI person quite well and the chief librarian—who deals with appeals."

It is important to stress that this compendium merely scratches the surface of the monumental levels of fraud that have been exposed as a result of the hacked emails.

People will look back on this moment as the beginning of the end for global warming alarmism and the agenda to implement draconian measures of regulation and control along with the levy of a global carbon tax.

Many more revelations will be forthcoming as a result of this leak, and the desperate effort on behalf of the establishment to whitewash the whole issue will only end up making the damage worse.

4

Americans Support an International Agreement to Reduce Global Warming

Anthony Leiserowitz

Anthony Leiserowitz is a research scientist at the School of Forestry and Environmental Studies at Yale University and the director of the Yale Project on Climate Change.

Most Americans believe that global warming is happening, that it is caused by human activity, that strong legislation is warranted to reduce carbon emissions, and that an international climate change treaty would be a good way to bring about the necessary reductions in emissions.

Overall, a large majority of the American public is personally convinced that global warming is happening (71%). Surprisingly, however, only 48 percent believe that there is consensus among the scientific community, while 40 percent of Americans still believe there is a lot of disagreement among scientists over whether global warming is occurring. Thus, many Americans appear to have already made up their minds, without waiting for a perceived scientific consensus. Further, 69 percent of Americans now believe that global warming is caused mainly by human activities (57%), or caused equally by humans and natural changes (12%), while only 29 percent believe it is caused mostly by natural changes in the environment.

Anthony Leiserowitz, *American Opinions on Global Warming: A Yale University/Gallup/ClearVision Institute Poll*, Yale University, July 23–26, 2007. Reproduced by permission.

Americans are evenly split, however, on their level of worry about global warming, with 50 percent personally worried either a great deal (15%) or a fair amount (35%) vs. 50 percent worried only a little (28%) or not at all (22%). These levels of personal worry are due in part to the fact that many Americans believe global warming is a serious threat to other species, people and places far away, but not so serious of a threat to themselves, their own families, or local communities.

Over the past few years, American perceptions that global warming is currently or will soon have dangerous impacts on people around the world have increased significantly. This survey found that 48 percent of Americans now believe that global warming is already having dangerous impacts on people (30%) or will within the next ten years (18%): a 20 percentage point increase since the question was last asked in a nationally representative survey in June, 2004. Surprisingly, a large majority of Americans (62%) now believe that global warming is an urgent threat requiring immediate and drastic action.

Americans Favor a Strong Climate Treaty

For example, a large majority of Americans (68%) now favor, at least in principle, an international treaty that goes far beyond the Kyoto Protocol, to require the United States to cut its emissions of carbon dioxide 90% by the year 2050.

The U.S. Congress is currently debating an increase in the fuel economy standard for cars, trucks, and SUV's. This survey found that a very large majority of Americans (85%) support a fuel economy standard of 35 miles per gallon, *even if a new car thus cost up to $500 more to buy*. Congress is also currently debating whether to mandate that electric utilities produce a certain percentage of their electricity from renewable energy sources. This survey found that 82 percent of Americans support legislation that requires utilities to produce at least 20% of their electricity from renewables, *even if it cost the average*

27

household an extra $100 a year. Additionally, 89 percent of Americans would support a requirement that all new homes and commercial buildings meet higher energy efficiency standards.

When asked if the United States could take actions to help reduce global warming, 87 percent of Americans strongly (66%) or somewhat agreed (21%).

However, this survey also found continued strong opposition to carbon taxes, such as higher taxes on electricity, with 71 percent of Americans strongly (49%) or somewhat opposed (22%), or higher taxes on gasoline, with 67 percent of Americans strongly (48%) or somewhat opposed (19%). Thus paradoxically, while Americans strongly support national and international action on global warming, and are willing to pay more for a car and on their yearly electric bill, they remain adamantly opposed to higher gasoline or electricity taxes.

Global warming is also emerging as an important issue in the [2008] presidential election. Survey respondents were asked: "If the presidential election were held today, how important would a candidate's position on global warming be in your decision about whom to vote for?" A surprising 40 percent of Americans said a candidate's position would be either extremely (16%) or very important (24%), with an additional 35 percent saying it would be somewhat important.

Finally, in the past, some commentators have suggested that many Americans feel either personally helpless to reduce global warming or to believe that the actions of a single country like the United States won't make any difference. This survey asked respondents if they could personally take actions to help reduce global warming and found that 82 percent of Americans strongly (55%) or somewhat agreed (27%). Likewise, when asked if the United States could take actions to help reduce global warming, 87 percent of Americans strongly

(66%) or somewhat agreed (21%). Further, 69 percent of Americans said they strongly (49%) or somewhat disagreed (20%) that the action of a single person won't make any difference in reducing global warming. Finally, 76 percent said they strongly (59%) or somewhat disagreed (17%) that the actions of a single country like the United States won't make any difference in reducing global warming. These results demonstrate that most Americans maintain a "can-do" attitude about this issue and believe that they individually and collectively as a nation can make an important difference in reducing global warming.

Overall, these results demonstrate that most Americans now believe that global warming is occurring, is caused by human activities, and is an urgent threat requiring immediate action. Only half, however, personally worry about global warming, largely because many believe it will primarily impact people, other species, and places far away. Nonetheless, they strongly support a number of national and international policies to address this problem, but remain strongly opposed to carbon taxes. With the presidential primaries and general election near, presidential candidates should recognize that global warming has become an important issue for the electorate. Finally, Americans remain optimistic and confident that they individually and collectively as a nation can make a difference.

How the Survey Was Conducted

This survey was conducted July 23–26, 2007, using telephone interviews with 1,011 adults, aged 18+. Respondents were drawn from Gallup's household panel, which was originally recruited through random selection methods. The CASRO [Council of American Survey Research Organizations] response rate was 40%. The final sample was weighted to be representative of U.S. adults nationwide. For results based on the total sample, one can say with 95% confidence that the margin of sampling error is ±4 percentage points.

5

The US Should Support International Efforts to Pass a Climate Treaty

The Union of Concerned Scientists

The Union of Concerned Scientists is a science-based nonprofit that works to develop innovative solutions and to secure responsible changes in government policy, corporate practices, and consumer choices. Its areas of interest include climate change, green vehicles, and green energy.

The Copenhagen Accord created a voluntary framework within which individual countries can work to reduce global warming emissions. The world is watching closely to see what kind of progress the United States makes. Congress has a role to play in moving climate negotiations forward, by passing domestic legislation that demonstrates US commitment. It is important that the emission targets America sets are comparable to those of other developed nations. Additionally, the country can provide funding to assist developing nations in acquiring clean energy technologies, as well as preventing deforestation. Negotiations to achieve a comprehensive international climate treaty provide the United States with an opportunity for renewed world leadership.

Negotiations to achieve international agreement on a global climate treaty are underway. During the December 2009 UN [United Nations] Framework Convention on Climate Change (UNFCCC) meeting in Copenhagen [Denmark],

The Union of Concerned Scientists, "The International Climate Treaty and U.S. Legislation," www.UCSUSA.org, November 9, 2009. Copyright © 2009 by the Union of Concerned Scientists. Reproduced by permission.

the Copenhagen Accord was created. The Accord is a voluntary framework in which countries can commit to their own emissions reduction plans. Negotiations towards a comprehensive international treaty that is legally-binding will continue through 2010 with the hopes of reaching such agreement in the future. These negotiations provide the United States with an excellent opportunity for renewed world leadership on clean technology, energy conservation, and global security. Moreover, international cooperation towards addressing climate change will provide additional opportunities for U.S. businesses that are focused on clean technology to thrive from exports.

Development of domestic climate and energy legislation and the international climate negotiations are running on a parallel schedule, which provides Congress with an opportunity to influence the outcome of the international process. The U.S. negotiators, appointed by the State Department, take their cues from Congress, because treaties must be voted on by the U.S. Senate and pass with a two-thirds majority to be ratified.

The United States should match the funding other developed nations have already provided for these efforts.

Since the development of the Copenhagen Accord, the world is watching U.S. climate policy closely. It is imperative that Congress quickly move a climate and energy bill toward becoming law to show the progress and commitment of the United States to helping prevent the worst effects of climate change. If the United States continues to make progress towards a strong domestic national climate policy simultaneous to the international process, other countries of the UNFCCC will be encouraged to increase their efforts towards reducing their own emissions.

Strong Domestic Policies Needed for International Success

It is crucial that the legislation developed by Congress is strong enough to provide the U.S. delegation a robust foundation from which to negotiate. To the international community, one of the most important factors of a U.S. climate and energy bill is deep reduction targets for U.S. global warming pollution. Specifically, the U.S. targets must be on par with those of other leading developed nations. Setting targets at these levels will indicate that the United States is truly committed to moving forward by reducing heat-trapping emissions and taking responsibility for our part in global warming. It will also help secure reciprocal action from key developing countries whose contribution to the global goal of reducing emissions is critical to avoiding dangerous climate change.

In addition to creating a plan to limit our global warming pollution domestically, providing funding to help developing countries reduce their pollution and adapt to global warming is the best way to encourage all nations to agree on global action.

US Cooperation Is Key to Success

The United States can demonstrate cooperation with developing nations in the following ways:

- Funding tropical forest protection in developing countries, which will help reduce global heat-trapping emissions as well as promote sustainable development. Tropical deforestation has been estimated to account for about 15 percent of the world's global warming pollution, and the world cannot fully address global warming without addressing this source.

- Funding international adaptation to help the world's most vulnerable peoples adjust to the effects of global warming from which they are already suffering. Adaptation actions will reduce or avoid tensions around such issues as water sources and food shortages, thus alleviating global security problems.

- Supporting the sharing and transfer of clean technology to developing countries will help these nations to lower their global warming pollution. U.S. businesses and green workers could benefit from the exports of clean technology.

This critical funding will demonstrate a vital commitment by Congress to the global effort to reduce heat-trapping emissions and support survival of the world's most vulnerable in the face of inevitable global warming impacts. The United States should match the funding other developed nations have already provided for these efforts. For example, Norway—a country with less than 5 million people—has provided $500 million per year, for five years, to reduce deforestation. In Copenhagen, the United States promised $1 billion over 3 years to reduce deforestation. This short-term financing shows leadership by the United States and must be followed up with long-term financing and climate legislation.

The House of Representatives passed the American Clean Energy and Security Act in late June 2009. This represents an important milestone, but the legislation must be strengthened as it moves through the Senate. The near-term emissions targets in this legislation must be improved to approach the targets adopted by other developed nations. The bill creates a limit on how much global warming pollution can be emitted. Companies must purchase permits from the government to emit specified amounts of pollution. This creates a financial incentive for companies to pursue clean, efficient technologies, because they can save money by purchasing fewer permits, or make money by selling their permits to other polluters. Under the bill, only 1 percent of the revenue from the sale of these permits is allocated for international funding for adaptation and clean technology, which must be increased. The international funding allocation for protection of tropical forests must be kept at 5 percent of the revenue. A stronger bill would create the conditions necessary to secure a robust international climate treaty. It would also foster a transition to a clean energy economy, which could form the basis of an economic recovery in the United States and abroad.

Next Steps for Congress

The United States must pass strong domestic legislation that addresses mitigation, adaptation, technology, and financing—the necessary pillars for addressing climate change on an international level. Furthermore, members of Congress and their staff should continue to engage substantively in the negotiations process as they did by attending UNFCCC meetings such as the Conference of Parties in Copenhagen. Both the international negotiations and the U.S. domestic process are reaching a critical point, and Congress can play a key role in achieving success on both fronts.

6

An International Climate Treaty Will Pose a Threat to US Sovereignty

The Washington Times

The Washington Times *is a daily interest newspaper published in Washington, D.C.*

If passed, the Copenhagen Climate Treaty will pose an onerous threat to US sovereignty and American liberties. It will create a Carbon Market Regulatory Agency with ultimate authority to regulate any industry that produces carbon emissions, including manufacturing, transportation, agriculture and mining, as well as energy production. The cost of the climate treaty is estimated to be $800 billion over five years—a massive transfer of funds from productive to unproductive areas of the world. Supporters of the Copenhagen Climate Treaty appeal to irrational and unsubstantiated fears, since average global temperatures have actually been falling since 1998.

Environmental alarmism is being exploited to chip away at national sovereignty. The latest threat to American liberties may be found in the innocuous sounding Copenhagen Climate Treaty, which will be discussed at the United Nations climate-change conference in mid-December [2009]. The alert was sounded on the treaty in a talk given by British commentator Lord Christopher Monckton at Bethel College in St. Paul, Minn., on Oct. 14. Video of the talk has become an Internet sensation.

The Washington Times, "EDITORIAL: Green World Government," October 27, 2009. Copyright © 2009 by Foster Reprints. Reproduced by permission.

The treaty's text is not yet finalized but its principles are aimed at regulating all economic activity in the name of climate security, with a side effect that billions of dollars would be transferred from productive countries to the unproductive.

The control lever is the regulation of carbon emissions, which some purport are causing global warming. The treaty would establish a Carbon Market Regulatory Agency and "global carbon budget" for each country.

The governing authority envisioned by the document reads like a bad George Orwell knockoff.

In effect, this would allow the treaty's governing bodies to limit manufacturing, transportation, travel, agriculture, mining, energy production and anything else that emits carbon—like breathing.

Appealing to Fear

Treaty supporters market the agreement through fear. Even though mean global temperatures have been on a downward spiral for several years after peaking in 1998, we are told that catastrophe is imminent. "The world has already crossed the threshold beyond which it is no longer possible to avoid negative impacts of anthropogenic climate change," says proposed treaty language being circulated by Greenpeace, the World Wildlife Fund and other groups. It is critical that they cultivate a sense of impending doom to justify the sweeping restrictions and new powers enshrined in the treaty. The sky is falling and they want us to act now, act swiftly, act before it is too late—but don't read the fine print.

The governing authority envisioned by the document reads like a bad [author] George Orwell knockoff. The treaty establishes a body called the Conference of the Parties (COP), which is given ultimate authority over administering and enforcing the treaty. Its executive arm is something called the

Adaptation Fund Board, under which is the Copenhagen Climate Facility, also known as "the Facility." The Facility is necessary because in order to save the planet, "the way society is structured will need to change fundamentally." This change would be impossible under the "fragmented set of existing institutions," so the Facility will step in with "such legal capacity as is necessary for the exercise of its functions and the protection of its interests." That's the Facility's interests, not yours.

The Facility will be run by an executive committee, the membership of which "may include representation from relevant intergovernmental and non-governmental stakeholders." So left-wing pressure groups, animal rights fanatics, tree-huggers, [former Vice President] Al Gore or any other part of the environmentalist fringe would be eligible for executive committee membership. Naturally, global-warming skeptics like Lord Monckton need not apply.

The environmental movement is driven by a millenarian determination to save humanity from itself, regardless of its impact on real people.

Authority to Tax Anything They Can Imagine

A "massive scaling up of financial resources" will be required to fund the COP's activities. The United States and others will be required to transfer $800 billion over five years, with additional funding requirements assessed on an as-needed basis. The COP will have taxing authority "including, but not limited to, a levy on aviation and maritime transport." The ability to tax aircraft and shipping is bad enough, but as careful readers of the elastic clauses of the U.S. Constitution know, the phrase "including but not limited to" authorizes any tax they can imagine.

Signatories of the treaty will be required to file reports to the Committee for Reporting and Review ("the Committee"), and if found not in compliance with the treaty's terms, they may have to face "the Facilitative Branch." If this branch finds that a country is violating the terms of the agreement, it will "undertake the measures necessary" to bring the country back into compliance.

The treaty language would be farcical but for the fanaticism of its proponents. The environmental movement is driven by a millenarian determination to save humanity from itself, regardless of its impact on real people. President [Barack] Obama reportedly will skip the Copenhagen meeting unless the treaty language is finalized. We urge him to resist the urge to pander to the international community at the expense of the United States.

We look forward to headlines about record cold temperatures during the December climate summit, and to hearing desperate speeches about stopping irresistible global warming during the signing ceremony, held during a blizzard.

7

The US Must Lead the Way Toward Climate Change Policy Reform

Samuel Thernstrom

Samuel Thernstrom is a fellow at the American Enterprise Institute for Public Policy Research (AEI) and co-director of the AEI Geoengineering Project, a program launched by the institute to counter global climate change through geoengineering.

A year into the Barack Obama administration, the dream of a successful global climate agreement seems as far out of reach as it was during the Bush years. President Obama campaigned on a pledge to engage in vigorous negotiations, working toward a new era of global cooperation on climate change. However, he has largely allowed the U.S. Congress to take the lead in crafting domestic climate legislation, with little real success. Fatal flaws in the effort to pass an international climate treaty, exempting developing countries from emissions reductions, make it unlikely that such an agreement can ever be approved in the United States.

Reading the climate-change news in recent weeks, one might wonder who won the last election.

The [Barack] Obama administration has rejected the Kyoto Protocol (ensuring it will expire), adopted some of former

Samuel Thernstrom, "The Quiet Death of the Kyoto Protocol," *The American: The Journal of the American Enterprise Institute*, November 5, 2009. Copyright © 2009 American Enterprise Institute for Public Policy Research. Reproduced with permission of *The American Magazine*, a national magazine of politics, business, and culture (www.american.com).

President George W. Bush's key positions in international climate negotiations, and demurred when asked about reports that the president has decided to skip the December [2009] climate summit in Copenhagen [Denmark]. United Nations climate negotiator Yvo de Boer has concluded that it is "unrealistic" to expect the conference to produce a new, comprehensive climate treaty—which also describes the once-fond hopes for passage of domestic climate legislation this year—or even in Obama's first term.

This is not how it was supposed to be.

Among all the things that President Bush did to infuriate environmentalists, none was more inexcusable than his rejection of the Kyoto Protocol in 2001, and it was assumed that Obama's election meant a triumphant American return to the Kyoto fold—symbolically, at least, if not literally. Backed by large majorities in both houses of Congress, Obama was widely expected to quickly pass a Kyoto-style domestic cap-and-trade program for greenhouse gases, positioning America to take the moral high ground in Copenhagen, thus luring (or compelling) China and India to accept emissions targets.

While Barack Obama did not explicitly campaign on a pledge to ratify Kyoto, his hope-and-change message was clear.

Bipartisan Rejection of Kyoto

The story, at least on the international side, is complicated by our actual history with Kyoto, which is not as simple as some greens would portray it today. Rejection of Kyoto—in 1997, three years before Bush's election—was a rare moment of bipartisan consensus on climate policy; the Senate voted unanimously (95-0) against its basic tenets, and the [President Bill] Clinton-[Vice-President Al] Gore administration never submitted it for ratification. (Even a little-known state legislator from Illinois named Barack Obama voted to condemn Kyoto and prohibit the state from regulating greenhouse gas emissions.)

The treaty's fundamental flaws were well understood: It set very ambitious—and costly—targets for the United States while allowing emissions from the developing world to continue to rise unchecked. (And indeed today, despite Kyoto's ratification, China has become the world's leading emitter of greenhouse gases.) Americans don't mind contributing to a solution, but Kyoto asked a lot of sacrifice for little reward.

Despite that moment of bipartisan consensus on Kyoto, the election of George W. Bush quickly made opposition to Kyoto indefensible among all right-thinking environmentalists; Kyoto's genuine structural flaws were excused, if not forgotten, by all but a few. And instead of it being Al Gore's fault for agreeing to a pie-in-the-sky treaty in defiance of a unanimous vote of the Senate, Kyoto's demise was blamed on Bush for his more forthright refusal in 2001 to seek ratification. This is natural in politics, of course, but the cost was a loss of focus on the need for effective alternatives to Kyoto.

As he has with a number of key issues, President Obama has let Congress largely take the lead in crafting domestic climate legislation.

A Message of Change

While Barack Obama did not explicitly campaign on a pledge to ratify Kyoto, his hope-and-change message was clear: *Elect me and America will no longer be an outcast on climate policy; I will lead the charge for a new, Kyoto-style agreement in Copenhagen.* And President-elect Obama's first statement on climate change was a bold pledge: "Once I take office, you can be sure that the United States will once again engage vigorously in these negotiations and help lead the world toward a new era of global cooperation on climate change." In retrospect, the commitment seems a bit vague, but his audience has no doubt what he meant. As one British newspaper breathlessly reported:

> Prospects for success in the world's struggle to combat global warming have been transformed at a stroke after U.S. President-elect Barack Obama made it clear that America would play its full part in renewing the Kyoto Protocol climate-change treaty. His words, in effect, brought an end to eight years of willful climate obstructionism by the administration of George Bush, who withdrew the U.S. from Kyoto in March 2001, thus doing incalculable damage to the efforts of the international community to construct a unified response to the threat.

Eleven months later, the dream of a successful global climate policy seems as far out of reach as ever, and America continues to have profound disagreements over climate policy with much of the world. In the good old days of the bad old Bush administration, it was easy to paper over the profoundly complicated and difficult obstacles to effective national and international climate agreements; "Blame Bush!" was a cry greens could all rally around. Today, the inconvenient truth of the matter is harder to hide, and to a surprising degree, the rallying cry for the rest of the world remains "Blame America!"

Inconvenient Truths

How did we reach this point, less than a year into the Obama administration? There are different dynamics at work: undue deference to Congress on domestic legislation, and insufficient leverage in international negotiations to overcome vastly dissimilar national interests and abilities.

As he has with a number of key issues, President Obama has let Congress largely take the lead in crafting domestic climate legislation—to his regret, one must imagine, seeing the results. The bill that passed the House by the narrowest of margins was a monstrosity by any measure, hailed even by its most fervent supporters as a detestable mess. Progress in the Senate has been far slower, and it is increasingly clear that no bill will pass this year. Hopes for action on climate will have to carry over to 2010—a contentious election year, at a time when unemployment may well top 10 percent and polling suggests that public concern about climate change is falling dramatically. The prospects for a bill in 2010 are not good— and Democrats are likely to lose seats in those elections, leaving them poorly positioned to pass legislation in 2011–12 as the next presidential election approaches.

Less than a year into Obama's first term, it seems plausible that no climate bill will pass before 2013 at the earliest, and that the Kyoto Protocol will expire in 2012 without a comprehensive successor agreement to take its place.

Clearly, the road to an agreement on climate that satisfies both domestic and international constituents will be long, at best.

Having promised to lead the Copenhagen negotiations to a successful conclusion, Obama now finds himself in a bind: Unable to get a bill through Congress, he doesn't want to repeat Gore's mistake of letting Europeans pressure him into signing a treaty the Senate won't ratify while sanctioning unrestricted emissions from the developing world. Since treaties require the support of two-thirds of the Senate, ratification will be more difficult than passage of domestic legislation. So the administration's draft implementing agreement submitted to the UN [United Nations] in May specified that emissions reductions would be subject to "conformity with domestic law." In other words, whatever is agreed to here doesn't mean a thing if the Senate doesn't agree. As Jonathan Pershing, a top State Department negotiator, remarked at the recent climate negotiators' meeting in Bangkok. "We are not going to be part of an agreement we cannot meet."

This position protects Obama from the danger of getting ahead of the Senate—while infuriating Europe and developing nations that consider strong American action on climate long overdue. As an anonymous European Commission official remarked in September, climate negotiations are "not going well":

> European Union officials have grown increasingly frustrated at the U.S. stance, saying it has fallen short on both its level of ambition to reduce emissions and on offering aid to developing nations. "So far, we thought the basic problem was the Chinese and the Indians. But now I think the problem appears to lie most clearly with the U.S."

The Road Will Be Long

Clearly, the road to an agreement on climate that satisfies both domestic and international constituents will be long, at best.

The China-India problem remains unsolved as well, and Obama clearly is not blind to the serious political, economic, and environmental problems with any treaty that reaffirms Kyoto's sanction of unrestricted emissions from developing countries. Climate advocates have long argued that the key to overcoming developing world resistance to emissions limits is American leadership; if we go first, China and India will follow. Skeptics note that what we gain in credibility we may lose in leverage needed to force a deal in Copenhagen. In any case, Congress's inaction—and its continued concern about trade competitiveness questions—has forced Obama, in effect, to take the Bush position: No new treaty without developing world participation. As NPR [National Public Radio] recently reported, Kyoto will be allowed to expire after 2012. "The United States never ratified the agreement because it doesn't require any action from the developing world, including

China, the world's largest emitter. The Bush administration considered that a fatal flaw. And so does the Obama White House."

This is the crux of the argument: The crucial feature of the deal that Gore struck in Kyoto was its exemption of the developing world from emissions reduction obligations. Without that concession, the developing world would never have accepted the treaty—but with it, the treaty was almost worthless (particularly since, as a political matter, that provision precluded American participation). This was the fatal flaw of Kyoto—and, having established that exemption, it will be doubly hard to persuade developing nations to undo it.

Obama apparently hopes to finesse these issues by reaching bilateral agreements with China and India, although critics complain that doing so would potentially undermine the multilateral architecture of the prospective Copenhagen treaty. But recent reports that no bilateral agreement will be announced during Obama's visit to China in November suggest that a deal by Copenhagen is unlikely. China and India are both under enormous international pressure to accept emissions limits—and even greater domestic pressure to maintain a strong rate of economic growth. Both countries have so far firmly resisted calls for binding emissions caps, although President Hu Jintao has said that China will cut its emissions relative to economic growth—that is, the greenhouse-gas "intensity" of the Chinese economy, not total emissions—by a "notable" margin by 2020.

The Administration Has Taken a Hard Line

Meanwhile, to its credit, the administration is taking a surprisingly hard line with developing countries. State Department envoy Todd Stern recently called on developing nations to make significant, binding commitments to emissions reductions, remarking:

We don't in the U.S. deny that we have real historical responsibility but the IEA [International Energy Agency] in Paris will tell you that 97 percent of the growth in emissions between now and 2050 will come from the developing world. The U.S. has to act and the EU [European Union] and Japan but also the developing countries. It's the only way to solve this problem.

This is strong stuff—and it runs contrary to much conventional liberal wisdom in the United States, Europe, and particularly in the developing world, which holds that the nations most responsible for past emissions should be primarily responsible for mitigation. If climate change is a moral issue (as most liberals insist), then the polluter responsible for past emissions should be on the hook for their consequences today; if we see the issue purely in pragmatic terms, then responsibility must be shared significantly with the major developing economies. The insistence that developing nations make credible commitments to emissions reductions has been a core conservative principle on climate; seeing Obama pick up that torch is encouraging—it is vital to crafting any true, effective global agreement—but it remains to be seen whether any combination of pressure and persuasion will be sufficient to strike a deal on those terms.

A new approach to climate policy will require a willingness to somehow rise above politics to challenge conventional liberal wisdom on key aspects of climate policy.

What should we make of the surprising Bushification of these aspects of Obama's climate policy? It is too soon to say. It is easy to see these events as a series of failures, yet they may still prove to be the first steps to success if the president is committed to crafting real alternatives. Certainly the first step to success lies in rejecting the failed approaches of the past—and inadvertently or not, Obama has moved further in that direction than might have been expected a year ago. On the international side, he has taken a surprisingly reformist stance. But building a new architecture for domestic and international climate policy would be an enormous undertaking.

A New, More Centrist Approach Is Needed

Doing so would require a willingness to challenge the cherished assumptions of many environmental advocates, a risky proposition for a president who has been increasingly forced to rely on his base for support. Yet the potential rewards are also great: if ever an issue cried out for a sensible, centrist approach, it is climate change.

One of the most frustrating aspects of the President Bush's climate policy was not its substantive flaws (although there were many), but rather that the president was such an inarticulate advocate for it. The president's greatest power is the bully pulpit, and if he uses it wisely, he can change the way America, and even the world, thinks about a complex issue like climate change. President Bush had that opportunity and squandered it; President Obama is better positioned to tackle the task, but healthcare and other matters have, so far, come first. The question is whether, as the president retrenches following a disappointing first year in office, he will be willing to take a gamble on a new approach to climate.

The odds against that scenario are tall; the smart—or at least, natural—political move for Obama would be to simply blame Republicans for blocking the climate bill, an easy charge to make, and both parties appear willing to take their positions to the voters. Yet a new approach to climate policy will require a willingness to somehow rise above politics to challenge conventional liberal wisdom on key aspects of climate policy. Doing so would not be easy for Obama in this intensely partisan time. But with polls indicating dwindling support for him from independents and Republicans, a creative, centrist approach to climate could be the key to turning that trend around.

There is a credible body of serious, creative work exploring different approaches to both domestic and international climate change issues; if, in the face of gridlock in Congress and the collapse of the Kyoto system, Obama chooses to make this issue a top priority, a fresh start on climate policy could still earn bipartisan support. Alas, what we have heard so far from President Obama is merely a pledge to "redouble" his efforts to strike a deal in Copenhagen—or, at least, to create a "framework for progress"—without acknowledging the genuinely thorny issues that have precluded agreement to date. Admitting failure is the first step to success—yet it violates the first rule of politics. Obama campaigned on a promise to change politics as usual in Washington and around the world. Can he do it on climate? Some commentators argue that the only problem with the legislation being considered by Congress is that it lacks sufficient votes for passage; in fact, its political problems are rooted in its structural flaws, not vice versa. An acknowledgment from President Obama that a new approach is needed would start a fresh conversation on climate that is long overdue.

8

President Obama Needs to Explore Other Climate Policy Options

Joseph Romm

Joseph Romm is the editor of the Climate Progress *blog, named by* TIME *Magazine* one of the top green websites in 2007. He is also a senior fellow at the Center for American Progress.

Republicans in the US Senate are united in their resolve to prevent ratification of a global climate treaty, which they say will damage the economy and lead to job losses. Since Republican opposition will make it impossible for a treaty to be passed, President Barack Obama needs to rethink his support for climate negotiations and explore other policy options that have a greater likelihood of leading to significant reductions in global temperatures.

It is all but inconceivable that [President Barack] Obama can deliver the 67 votes in the Senate needed to ratify a global climate treaty—no matter what happens in the 12 months between Poznan [a United Nations climate conference was held in Poznan, Poland, in 2008] and Copenhagen [climate conference in 2009 in Denmark]. And the only thing worse than no global climate treaty in 2009 is a treaty that Obama can't get ratified.

Yes, Democrats have expanded their majority in the Senate, edging closer and closer to the magical 60 votes needed to

Joseph Romm, "Obama Can't Get a Global Climate Treaty Ratified, So What Should He Do Instead?," *Grist Magazine*, December 2, 2008. Copyright © 2008 by Grist Magazine. Reproduced by permission.

stop filibusters. But the conservatives in Congress are stuck in 1985 (1885?), unwilling or unable to acknowledge the now painfully obvious reality of global warming or the remarkable advances that have been made in clean technologies.

Conservative Senators lined up as a solid block against the Boxer-Lieberman-Warner bill. Worse, the GOP [Republican party] seems to think that among all the losing issues they pushed in their historic drubbing at the polls, their "drill baby drill" message was actually a winner. As one post-election story put it

> But several prominent party officials said they believe the GOP's message is fundamentally sound when it comes to energy policy, pointing to that issue as one of the few political bright spots in recent years.

Again, that was not from an article by *The Onion.*

So even if there are 60 Senate votes to override a right-wing filibuster against a strong domestic climate bill, there aren't 67 votes for a new climate treaty.

The GOP has apparently borrowed their motto from [Charles Maurice] Talleyrand's comment on the dying French aristocracy, "They have learned nothing, and they have forgotten nothing." As I noted in "Notes from the conservative stagnation, Part 10," [an opinion piece published in *Grist Magazine* in November 2008] Grover Norquist, the president of Americans for Tax Reform, "suggested that some calls to update conservatism—by taking global warming more seriously, for instance—were essentially disguised calls to move the party to the left." He added, "They will be cheerfully ignored." Denial is bliss.

Every major conservative think tank remains fervently blind to reality. The major conservative pundits are equally blinkered.

So we can expect the vast majority of GOP Senators to keep beating the drums that any cap-and-trade bill—domestic or international—will raise energy prices and ruin the economy. We can expect repetitions of lines from the Senate debate last summer:

- Sen. James Inhofe, R-Okla.: "The vast majority of scientists do not believe that anthropogenic greenhouse gas emissions are a major contributor to climate change."

- Sen. Jon Kyl, R-Ariz.: This bill means "people must turn off air-conditioning in the summer."

- Sen. Saxby Chambliss, R-Ga.: "This bill will attack citizens at the pump" and "increase job losses."

- Sen. Jeff Sessions, R-Ala.: This bill will "leave us less competitive in the world marketplace."

- Sen. John Thune, R-S.D.: This bill "could bankrupt U.S. air carriers."

- Sen. Kit Bond, R-Mo.: "Nobody in their right mind" believes we can get half our power from wind and solar or drive a "fleet of golf carts."

Note that these attacks can be trotted out whether we are in a recession and energy prices are low or if we have recovered economically and energy prices are rising again.

So even if there are 60 Senate votes to override a right-wing filibuster against a strong domestic climate bill, there aren't 67 votes for a new climate treaty. And that means the UNFCCC [United Nations Framework Convention on Climate Change] process as we now know it is essentially a Dead Man Walking, even if nobody knows it yet.

Obama needs to think very hard about whether he is making promises he can't keep. International negotiators are now in Poland to figure out how to create a follow on to the Kyoto protocol in Copengagen next December [2009].

Last month [November 2008], Obama gave a surprise post-election climate address in which he directly said to delegates around the world headed to Poland that "your work is vital to the planet":

> And once I take office, you can be sure that the United States will once again engage vigorously in these negotiations, and help lead the world toward a new era of global cooperation on climate change.

We do need a new era of global cooperation on climate change. But Obama will need all of his eloquence and smarts—and that of his new exceptional Secretary of State—to figure out how to replace the UNFCCC process with something more viable. And he needs to think hard about the value of "engaging vigorously" in the negotiations of a global treaty he can't ratify.

The prize we must keep our eyes on, however, is not any particular process but a particular outcome—keeping total planetary warming to under 2°C warming from preindustrial levels.

9

President Obama Can Sign a Climate Treaty Without Senate Approval

Kate Sheppard

Kate Sheppard covers energy and environmental politics for Mother Jones magazine's Washington, D.C., bureau.

Environmental groups such as Greenpeace and the Center for Biological Diversity, frustrated by the US Senate's refusal to ratify the Kyoto Protocol, are arguing that President Barack Obama has the authority to enter into a climate agreement on his own, without Senate approval. Some legal experts agree, pointing out that the administration could enter into a binding climate agreement through an executive order and based on existing laws. For example, the Supreme Court has determined that the federal government can regulate greenhouse gas emissions under the Clean Air Act. While it is true that the legal framework for executive action exists, it may not be the best way to forge a lasting climate agreement.

In 1997, in the Japanese city of Kyoto, the [President Bill] Clinton administration agreed to a groundbreaking treaty to combat global warming. And that's when the trouble started. The Senate had unanimously refused to approve the Kyoto Protocol, and in the end the Clinton administration didn't even submit it for a vote in the upper chamber. This made the US both the world's biggest polluter and, ultimately,

Kate Sheppard, "Can Obama Sign a Climate Treaty Without Congress?" *Mother Jones*, December 18, 2009. Copyright © 2009 by Foundation for National Progress. Reproduced by permission.

the only industrialized nation to reject the accord. Now, as world leaders attempt to negotiate a new climate deal at Copenhagen [Denmark], environmentalists want to avoid a repeat of the Kyoto debacle. That's why some green groups are urging [President Barack] Obama to do an end-run around the Senate and assert that his presidential powers empower him to commit the US to a climate treaty on his own.

The EPA's ruling, as well as new rules that it is expected to release, enable Obama to sign an international accord with or without congressional approval, CBD argues.

Under Article II of the constitution, a president can sign an international treaty, but it must by ratified by two-thirds of the Senate before it becomes law. But there are also other types of international accords, like trade deals, that can be entered via a congressional-executive agreement, which requires only the approval of a simple majority in both houses of Congress. There's no ironclad rule that determines which international pacts fall into which category. But neither route is easy. The last treaty to win ratification was the Strategic Offensive Reductions Treaty in 2002, which reduced the nuclear arsenals of Russia and US. Trade agreements are no picnic, either—the most recent pact approved was with Peru in 2007, while [President George W.] Bush administration deals with Colombia, South Korea and Panama are still languishing on Capitol Hill. When you consider that a domestic cap-and-trade bill has yet to win backing from the 60 senators required to even bring the measure up for a vote, the chances of securing 67 supporters for a major international treaty seem very slim indeed.

Against that backdrop, some environmental groups and legal experts are calling on Obama to take unilateral action. At a briefing in Copenhagen last week [December 2009], Greenpeace and the Center for Biological Diversity (CBD), an

Arizona-based conservation group, argued that the president could become a party to a binding climate agreement simply by signing an executive agreement, bypassing Congress altogether. There is "very solid legal footing for negotiating an executive agreement here in Copenhagen," argued Kassie Siegel, senior counsel of CBD, which has issued a new report outlining what it sees as Obama's legal options for entering a climate accord. Friends of the Earth [FOE] has also endorsed this concept. "If he wants to lead the world on climate change, he has to step up to the plate and commit the US to the treaty process," said FOE president Erich Pica.

Some legal experts have also made the case that the president does not need the approval of 67 senators before joining a global effort to stop planet-warming pollution.

The president has full authority to sign a climate treaty on his own, CBD argues, because Congress has already granted him the domestic power to regulate emissions. In making this claim, CBD is referring to a number of federal laws, most notably the Clean Air Act. In early December the Environmental Protection Agency (EPA) issued a final declaration that greenhouse gases are a threat to human health and can be regulated under the 1990 amendments to the legislation. The EPA's ruling, as well as new rules that it is expected to release, enable Obama to sign an international accord with or without congressional approval, CBD argues.

CBD also cites the Global Climate Protection Act of 1987—a largely forgotten law that empowers the president to "identify technologies and activities to limit mankind's adverse effect on the global climate" by "slowing the rate of increase of concentrations of greenhouse gases in the atmosphere in the near term" and "developing and proposing to Congress a coordinated national policy on global climate change." This 1987 legislation also states that the "Secretary of

State shall be responsible to coordinate those aspects of United States policy requiring action through the channels of multilateral diplomacy, including the United Nations Environment Program and other international organizations."

Some legal experts have also made the case that the president does not need the approval of 67 senators before joining a global effort to stop planet-warming pollution. Michael B. Gerrard, a professor at the Center for Climate Change Law at Columbia University's law school, recently wrote that the administration could enter a binding international climate pact via an executive agreement combined with the existing authority granted to him under domestic law. Michael Widmore, the executive director of the Institute for Policy Integrity at New York University School of Law has echoed this view, noting that a section of the Clean Air Act authorizes the president "to enter international agreements . . . and to develop standards and regulations which protect the stratosphere." He concluded: "This could provide a foundation for an executive agreement—and Obama wouldn't need to round up 60 votes from the Senate."

Other environmental groups warn that trying to act on climate without Congress could be politically disastrous.

But even if this course of action is legally feasible, is it actually a good idea? It's true that the Supreme Court has determined that the federal government can regulate greenhouse gas emissions under the Clean Air Act. But the administration, Congress, and most of the environmental community has stated a preference for a new federal law that specifically deals with carbon dioxide pollution. That's because only so much can be done to reduce emissions using EPA rules alone.

EPA regulation does not provide the timing or certainty on emissions cuts that other nations are seeking from the US at Copenhagen. For starters, current EPA regulations lack any firm targets about the size of carbon dioxide cuts or a deadline for making reductions. And because such rules are usually implemented in phases, action would probably be slow. EPA regulations would also likely be the target of a deluge of lawsuits, potentially causing long delays and making it harder for other nations to count on US commitments. Nor could EPA rules be used to create mechanisms for financing adaptation and mitigation, seen as essential to any final climate accord. "The sort of international agreement that the United States could be part of while using EPA regulation to deliver on its commitments—that is, an agreement that wouldn't require Senate or Congressional approval—would look radically different from what most of the negotiators gathered in Denmark have in mind," wrote Michael Levi of the Council on Foreign Relations.

Siegel of the CBD acknowledged that a legislative solution would be "the best way to go." But she observed that the "Senate has been standing in the way for 12 years now," and Obama should not feel compelled to wait. She added: "What we are saying is he is not legally constrained here."

But other environmental groups warn that trying to act on climate without Congress could be politically disastrous. "He can do a lot of things that a lot of groups want to see him do—if he's willing to see it kill the Senate [cap-and-trade] bill," argued Alden Meyer, director of strategy and policy for the Union of Concerned Scientists. "That's the political reality."

A solid bloc of Senate Democrats is still unwilling to support a domestic cap-and-trade measure, and at least one has already objected to the mere idea of Obama making nonbinding commitments at Copenhagen to targets that weren't previously approved by the upper chamber. Then there are the Republicans seeking to torpedo climate action outright. On Thursday [December 17, 2009] Sen. James Inhofe briefly touched down in Copenhagen to inform the international community that the US Congress won't support climate legislation. "You don't want to feed into that," said Meyer. A glimpse of the likely GOP line of attack could be viewed in a rather audacious January op-ed by John Yoo and John Bolton—hardly shrinking violets on the subject of expansive presidential powers. The pair warned that Obama may seek to sidestep the Senate and sign a climate treaty alone, and that such a course of action would be an unacceptable threat to the Senate's constitutional authority.

And the risks aren't purely political. Getting into a turf war with the Senate could result in very real setbacks for Obama's environmental agenda. Senate Republicans have already tried once this year to cut off funding to the EPA to prevent it from regulating carbon, and could easily do so again. In addition, if a climate accord hasn't been ratified by the Senate but is instead implemented via regulations, it could be more easily reversed by Congress or a future president. "The international community has to have the assurance that any commitment by the United States is negotiated on behalf of the country as a whole, and will be lived up to," said Matthias Duwe, director of the Climate Action Network Europe. "It would be detrimental if there was a rollback afterwards."

While CBD acknowledges that it's rare for the US to enter an international pact through a sole executive agreement, it argues that there "is no real dispute" that this type of agreement is binding under international law. But the report provides only a handful of precedents. Some are old (such as 1937 and 1941 agreements with the Soviet Union), and others deal with an extremely unusual or urgent situation (like the Iran hostage crisis). There's also the question of the legal precedent that would be established by such a move. One of the biggest criticisms of the Bush administration from the left was its aggressive drive to expand executive power, particularly in the national security realm, without appropriate consultation with Congress. If Obama acted alone on climate, it could enable future presidents to follow his example in other areas of foreign policy.

If the US and the rest of the world has learned anything from the Kyoto process, it's that it's perilous for an administration to promise policies that will trigger a revolt on Capitol Hill. "It's not wise for the executive branch to make agreements that go way beyond what they could expect Congress to go along with," said David Doniger, who served as the director of climate change policy at the Environmental Protection Agency during the Clinton administration and is now policy director of the climate center at the Natural Resources Defense Council.

Still, certain US climate activists insist that the time has come for Obama to deliver big in Copenhagen. Said Steve Herz, climate finance adviser at Greenpeace, "This is precisely the kind of difficult decision we elected him to make."

10

There Is Global Support for a Climate Change Treaty

World Public Opinion.org

WorldPublicOpinion.org is a project of the Program on International Policy Attitudes at the University of Maryland. It gathers information about the values and views of people in specific nations around the world, as well as global patterns of world public opinion.

Global opinion solidly favors the idea that climate change is a real and urgent problem. Opinion is divided over whether developing nations should be required to limit emissions, and whether developed countries should be required to provide aid to developing countries in exchange for commitments to limit emissions.

An international poll finds widespread agreement that climate change is a pressing problem. This majority, however, divides over whether the problem of global warming is urgent enough to require immediate, costly measures or whether more modest efforts are sufficient.

The survey was conducted by The Chicago Council on Global Affairs and WorldPublicOpinion.org in cooperation with polling organizations around the world. It includes 17 countries—China, India, the United States, Indonesia, Russia, Thailand, Ukraine, Poland, Iran, Mexico, South Korea, the Philippines, Australia, Argentina, Peru, Israel, Armenia—and the Palestinian territories. These represent more than 55 percent of the world population. . . .

WorldPublicOpinion.org, "Poll Finds Worldwide Agreement That Climate Change Is a Threat," March 13, 2007. Copyright © 2007 by the Program on International Policy Attitudes. Reproduced by permission.

Not all questions were asked in all countries.

Twelve countries were asked whether steps should be taken to address climate change and majorities in all but one of them favored action. The largest majority in favor of measures to combat global warming is found in Australia (92%).

China and Israel are the next most likely (83%) to favor such measures. Eighty percent of respondents in the United States—the world's largest emitter of greenhouse gases—also support taking such measures. The lowest level of support for taking steps to address the problem is found in India, nonetheless nearly half (49%) favor taking action while just 24 percent oppose it (26% do not answer).

In no country (out of 12 asked) does more than one in four endorse the statement, "Until we are sure that global warming is really a problem, we should not take any steps that would have economic costs." The countries where the highest percentages favor delaying any action are India (24%), Russia (22%) and Armenia (19%). The countries with the lowest are Argentina (3%), and Thailand (7%).

A separate question, asked in 10 countries, allowed respondents to evaluate the threat posed by "global warming" in the next ten years. Strong majorities in all of the countries say such climate change is an important threat with only small minorities calling it unimportant. The highest percentages of climate change skeptics are found in Armenia (16%) and Israel (15%).

In no country (out of 12 asked) does more than one in four endorse the statement, "Until we are sure that global warming is really a problem, we should not take any steps that would have economic costs."

While majorities in all countries agree that the threat posed by global warming is at least important, there is less agreement over whether it is critical. Majorities call it critical in

Mexico (70%), Australia (69%), South Korea (67%), Iran (61%), Israel (52%), and India (51%). Pluralities agree in Armenia (47%), China (47%) and the United States (46%). Ukraine is the only country divided about whether the problem is critical (33%) or important but not critical (33%).

Differences Over How Much to Spend

There is general agreement in 12 countries, as discussed above, that steps must be taken to address the problem of global warming, though there are differences over how much should be spent. In five countries, the most common view is: "Global warming is a serious and pressing problem. We should begin taking steps now even if this involves significant costs." These include: Australia (69%), Argentina (63%), Israel (54%), the United States (43%), and Armenia (37%).

In another five countries, the most commonly held opinion is: "The problem of global warming should be addressed, but its effects will be gradual, so we can deal with the problem gradually by taking steps that are low in cost." The countries endorsing a go-slow, low-cost approach are the Philippines (49%), Thailand (41%), Poland (39%), Ukraine (37%) and India (30%).

In two countries, the public is evenly divided between those who favor less expensive measures and those who believe the problem merits action involving significant cost: China (low cost 41%, significant costs 42%) and Russia (low costs 34%, significant costs 32%).

In Peru, only those who indicated they were informed about climate change—39 percent of the total sample—were asked whether steps should be taken to address the problem. Among these respondents, 92 percent favor action, including 69 percent who favor taking steps even if they involve significant costs.

Support for Developing Nations

Some governments, such as China's and India's, have argued that developing countries should not be obliged to limit greenhouse gas emissions as they struggle to catch up with the highly industrialized economies of Western Europe and the United States. The developing world, such countries say, releases far less CO_2 [carbon dioxide] and other greenhouse gasses per capita than do industrialized nations, whose cumulative emissions over the past century have caused the current problem.

Some have proposed that an equitable approach would be for developed nations to provide aid to developing nations if they would agree to impose some limits on their emissions. Publics in five developing countries were asked, "If the developed countries are willing to provide substantial aid, do you think the less-developed countries should make a commitment to limit their greenhouse gas emissions?" In all of five countries, majorities or pluralities say they should.

In Asia, the Chinese support environmental standards by an overwhelming 85 percent.

Most significantly, this includes a very large 79 percent majority of Chinese respondents and nearly half of those polled in India (48% agree, 29% disagree, 23% no answer). Majorities in Argentina (68%) and Armenia (63%) also concur. Results in Thailand are similar to those in India: about half of Thai respondents (49%) agree and only 9 percent disagree, though large numbers (43%) are uncertain.

China, India, Argentina, Armenia and Thailand are among the 169 countries that have ratified or accepted the Kyoto Protocol on climate change. They are not, however, considered industrialized countries under the treaty, which means they are not legally obliged to cut back emissions of CO_2 or other pollutants.

The survey also asked respondents in three developed countries whether developed countries should provide "substantial aid" to less-developed countries that "make a commitment to limit their greenhouse gas emissions." Respondents in all three show a high level of support for providing such assistance: 64 percent of Americans, 84 percent of Poles, and 72 percent of Ukrainians.

The United States, Poland and Ukraine are all considered Annex 1 or industrialized countries under the Kyoto accord, which means they are obligated to reduce emissions. Poland and Ukraine have both ratified the Kyoto Protocol; the United States has signed but refused to ratify it.

General Concern About the Global Environment

The survey also finds that world publics are very concerned about the global environment in general. Seven countries were asked to rate the importance of a number of foreign policy goals, including "improving the global environment." Overwhelming majorities in all seven countries rate improving the global environment as at least an "important" goal and majorities in all call it a "very important" one: Australia, 99 percent (very 88%); South Korea, 96 percent (very 60%); the United States 93 percent (very 54%), Armenia 86 percent (very 54%), China, 85 percent (very 54%); Thailand, 83 percent (very 61%); and India, 79 percent (very 51%).

Respondents were also asked whether "international trade agreements should or should not be required to maintain minimum standards for protection of the environment." In all 10 countries where this question was asked, very large majorities believe such standards should be required while in one country views are divided. Those in favor of standards include developing countries, whose governments have sometimes resisted environmental regulations, arguing that implementing such costly rules would put their economies at a competitive disadvantage.

In Asia, the Chinese support environmental standards by an overwhelming 85 percent. Seven in ten Thais (69%) also favor such standards as do six in ten Indians (60%).

In Latin America, an overwhelming majority of Argentines (90%) say such standards should be required. There is also strong support in Mexico (76%), where the North American Free Trade Agreement (NAFTA) has required the government to enact certain environmental measures. In Eastern Europe, environmental measures are favored in Poland (90%), Ukraine (88%) and Armenia (82%), both of which suffer from severe air and water pollution as well as deforestation dating from the Soviet era.

Support for environmental standards is also strong among the relatively wealthy publics of Israel (93%) and the United States (91%).

11

An International Climate Treaty Is Needless and May Harm the Economy

Ben Lieberman

Ben Lieberman is a senior policy analyst in the area of energy and the environment for the Thomas A. Roe Institute for Economic Policy Studies at The Heritage Foundation.

Since the Copenhagen Climate Conference in December 2009, it appears that progress on a climate treaty has stalled. There are two good reasons why this has happened: First, developing nations have insisted that the West is responsible for most emissions up to this point, and have declined to accept responsibility for reducing future emissions. However, nations such as China, which are developing rapidly, will be responsible for a much larger percentage of the share of emissions in the future, and must be included in any agreed-on schedules. Second, public support for a climate treaty has fallen off in recent months, due to increased concerns about jobs and the economy, as well the "climategate" scandal, which has cast doubt on the scientific basis for concerns about global warming.

The United Nations' first significant global warming meeting since last December's [2009] Copenhagen [Denmark] summit just wrapped up in Bonn [Germany, on April 1, 2010], with no progress toward a new international treaty to replace the Kyoto Protocol. This meeting was supposed to help lay the

Ben Lieberman, "U.N. Global Warming Treaty Process Still Off-Track in Bonn—and for Good Reason," *Heritage Foundation WebMemo No. 2880*, April 23, 2010. Copyright © 2010 The Heritage Foundation. Reproduced by permission.

groundwork for an agreement at the next major conference scheduled for Cancun, Mexico, in December. However, none of the issues that doomed negotiations in Copenhagen have been resolved, and it looks very unlikely that the process will be fixed this year.

But what is bad news for the U.N. [United Nations] climate treaty negotiators is good news for the rest of the world, as a new treaty would be an economically ruinous solution to what is increasingly looking like a non-problem.

Developed and Developing Nations Still Far Apart

Developing nations blame the West—and particularly the United States—for emitting most of the carbon dioxide and other greenhouse gases currently in the atmosphere. For that reason, representatives of these nations have demanded that they remain exempt from any obligations to reduce emissions.

Any new treaty to replace the existing Kyoto Protocol and provide post-2012 targets and timetables must either include developing nations or be wholly ineffective in achieving the goal of emissions reductions.

The 1997 Kyoto Protocol required 5 percent emissions reductions from developed nation signatories based on 1990 baseline emissions. But the treaty left developing nations off the hook. Kyoto's provisions expire in 2012, and perhaps the single biggest controversy as the U.N. attempts to fashion a post-Kyoto treaty is the treatment of the developing world. China, India, and other developing countries insist that they should maintain their exemptions in any post-2012 deal. In addition, many have demanded substantial foreign aid packages to deal with the consequences of warming.

The developing world is correct that the West was the first to industrialize and is historically responsible for most of the emissions, but this point is not relevant from a policy perspective. The reality looking forward is that quickly developing nations—chiefly China—will be responsible for the lion's share of future emissions. In fact, developing-world emissions surpassed those of the developed world in 2005 and are projected to rise at a rate seven times faster in the decades ahead. China alone out-emits the U.S., and its emissions are projected to increase nine times faster through 2030.

Thus, any new treaty to replace the existing Kyoto Protocol and provide post-2012 targets and timetables must either include developing nations or be wholly ineffective in achieving the goal of emissions reductions. To its credit, the U.S. delegation has been clear that a new agreement must have meaningful involvement from China and other high-emitting developing nations.

At the same time treaty negotiators continue to try to sell the world on a costly new agreement . . . the very reason for it—global warming—is proving to be less and less of a threat.

What emerged from Copenhagen, and is still true in Bonn, is that developing nations refuse to budge on accepting targets and timetables for reducing emissions. In addition, many of these nations expect increased foreign aid from the developed world and reacted angrily to suggestions from the U.S. delegation in Bonn that such aid be tied to accepting obligations to reduce emissions.

This impasse is unlikely to be narrowed in time for Cancun [a meeting scheduled for December 2010], if ever.

Public Skepticism Is Growing

At the same time treaty negotiators continue to try to sell the world on a costly new agreement in the midst of an ongoing global recession, the very reason for it—global warming—is proving to be less and less of a threat.

Although U.N. bureaucrats in Bonn ignored growing doubts about the scientific justification for their actions—just as they did in Copenhagen—waning public support is reaching a level where it cannot be ignored. In the U.S., recent surveys show concern over global warming dropping—one poll showed it finishing 20th out of 20 issues in terms of importance, while another had it finishing eight out of eight environmental issues.

Those same surveys show the economy and jobs to be the top priorities, which is precisely what a new global warming agreement would jeopardize. A Heritage Foundation analysis of the Waxman-Markey cap-and-trade bill, which passed the House last June [2009], found gross domestic product losses of over $9.4 trillion by 2035, over a million net job losses, and household energy cost increases exceeding $1,000 per year. A global treaty with similarly stringent provisions would impose comparable burdens.

The skepticism is spreading around the globe. For example, the "climategate" scandal—evidencing gross exaggeration and possibly outright fraud in the very U.N. scientific report that forms the basis of treaty negotiations—has been far more aggressively reported in Europe than in America and has impacted opinion there. Developing nations have also signaled their lack of any real concern over global warming by their unwillingness to undertake any sacrifices, even small ones, in the name of addressing it.

Beyond questions about the seriousness of global warming are questions about whether an international treaty would do any good. The Kyoto Protocol has thus far harmed the economies of European and other developed nation signatories but has not reduced emissions. In other words, a new global warming treaty is shaping up to be much more trouble than it is worth and is increasingly becoming a heavy lift politically.

Reality Check

Reality is creeping into the U.N. climate negotiations—the reality that China and other rapidly developing nations are unwilling to check their growing emissions and that the public does not see global warming as a serious threat justifying costly action. This reality is not going to go away by December. In fact, it may intensify into 2011.

12

Experts Are Pessimistic About Achieving an International Climate Treaty

Damian Carrington et al.

Damian Carrington, Suzanne Goldenberg, Juliette Jowit, Jonathan Watts, Alok Jha, James Randerson, David Smith, David Adam, and Tom Hennigan of the guardian.co.uk, the website of the Guardian *and* Observer *newspapers, all contributed to this article.*

Weeks after the end of the Copenhagen climate change summit in December 2009, experts believe the momentum toward an international climate agreement has faltered. A long list of problems have impeded progress: the United States has not shown a willingness to be a party to a binding agreement; China and India are not clearly committed to compromise; and the European Union has failed to follow through with the leadership it provided early on. Failure to reach an agreement has occurred in spite of the belief on the part of many parties to the talks that action must be taken soon to prevent catastrophic outcomes.

In the tense run-up to the Copenhagen climate change summit in December [2009], a senior British diplomat warned the *Guardian*: "We can go into extra time, but we can't afford a replay." At the end of the chaotic summit, that replays—in Mexico in November [2010]—was seen as a good result, given how close the entire show came to collapsing.

But now, just six weeks since the summit reached its dramatic but disappointing conclusion, senior figures around the world do not even believe the rematch is likely to be played.

Little Chance of an Agreement, Experts Say

Dozens of politicians, diplomats, economists, scientists and campaigners contacted by the *Guardian* agreed that while a global, legally binding treaty remains by far the best way to prevent global warming wreaking havoc on our civilisation, the chances of that treaty being achieved in 2010 are almost nil.

The energy has gone out of the negotiations, said some, with the momentum that drew well over 100 global leaders to the Danish capital in search of a deal now lost. The UN [United Nations] Framework Convention on Climate Change, which runs the negotiations, has drifted into a procedural vacuum and its head, Yvo de Boer, has lost all credibility, said others.

If global greenhouse gas emissions did begin to decline by the end of the decade, the world might be on a path to a relatively safe future.

The list of problems cited was long: the US political machine is unlikely to pass the climate laws other countries want as proof of intent; the willingness of China and India, the new climate change superpowers, to compromise is unclear; the erstwhile climate change leader, the European Union, is failing to lead. And all the while, what climate secretary Ed Miliband yesterday called the "siren voices" of climate sceptics sing more loudly, encouraged by leaked emails and dodgy details in important reports.

Simon Retallack, head of climate change at the Institute for Public Policy Research, reflected the thoughts of many: "We need to be honest and recognise that the national political conditions in the countries that matter most on climate change just weren't conducive to a deal in Copenhagen and if anything they have become worse since."

Positive Outlooks on the Part of Some

Nonetheless, some of those contacted resolutely retained the positive outlook expressed before Copenhagen. "The Japanese government would like to continue to work very hard for a legally binding agreement in Mexico," said a senior member of the country's negotiating team. But caveats were added: "We still have to coordinate with other governments and parties about the details."

The official UK [United Kingdom] position, from the Department of Energy and Climate Change, is similar: "The UK wants a comprehensive, legally binding climate change framework under the UN . . . and we are still determined to do everything we can to get a treaty agreed at the Mexico talks in November. Whilst the challenges are considerable—as shown in Copenhagen—we don't think it's right to lower our ambitions."

The most positive voices talked up the three-page document which emerged from the Copenhagen scrum. "We have an agreement—the Copenhagen accord—it covers all major countries and 80% of all emissions," said a senior UK climate official. "Our analysis of the commitments at their maximum extent is a peaking of emissions by 2020."

If global greenhouse gas emissions did begin to decline by the end of the decade, the world might be on a path to a relatively safe future. But the 20–30 nations meeting the "soft" UN deadline that expired last night have only tabled their minimum offers. For example, the European Union's promise of a move from a 20% to a 30% cut by 2020 remains contingent on the promises of others, an inducement that spectacularly failed to produce a breakthrough in Copenhagen.

Politically Binding Commitments May Be Enough

Some officials are now asking who needs a legally binding treaty anyway, with nations committing to "politically binding" individual action through domestic policies. Steve Howard, chief executive officer of the influential Climate Group, which promotes the low-carbon economy, reflected that view: "Is anyone really going to arrest any signatories to the [legally binding] Kyoto protocol for non-compliance?"

But a legally binding treaty, brokered by the UNFCCC [United Nations Framework Convention on Climate Change] remains the sole goal for many. "We recognise that there are difficult issues to be resolved, but we cannot see any other way to find a resolution," said Joanne Yawitch, the South African government's deputy director-general for environmental quality.

Tom Picken, international climate campaigner for Friends of the Earth, said building a "bottom-up" deal from individual nations' actions mean the carbon cuts scientists say are needed cannot be guaranteed or be fairly distributed. "We need to see a top-down cap set by science and equity considerations instead of domestic and bilateral deals."

Without the US, There Can Be No Treaty

The most important domestic action, along with China, is that of the US. "If we want an international treaty we have to have the US in there," said Janos Pasztor, [UN Secretary-General] Ban Ki-Moon's climate change adviser. Even senior US politicians echo the message: "If the United States doesn't move, I don't see a treaty on the cards," said Senator John Kerry, the Democrat who is fighting the uphill battle to get strong climate laws through Congress.

Engaging the world's current biggest polluter, China, is just as crucial.

But if the US difficulties are at least clear, China's position is not even that.

Conservative MP [Member of Parliament] Greg Clark, the UK's shadow secretary of state for climate change, said: "We need to understand why it was that countries like China considered a global deal to be against their interests."

Li Yan, Greenpeace China's climate campaigner said: "Looking back to Copenhagen, you can tell that the Chinese government wanted Copenhagen to be a success. But it did not go as the Chinese government wanted and gave lessons to decision makers. Copenhagen shows how big the pressure is on China and it is likely to grow. They need a new strategy."

One Chinese commentator said their problem was neither China or the US, as their positions were fixed. Yang Fuqiang, director of global climate solutions at WWF [World Wildlife Fund] said: "The key issue now is the EU [European Union]. Privately, the EU says it will adopt a 30% target and give $10bn [billion] to developing nations immediately. That can help. The EU has to take leadership."

Serious Reason for Concern

The urgent need for governments to stimulate economic growth was seen by business leaders as one way in which national action on carbon emissions could be driven in the absence of a global deal. Rhian Kelly, head of climate change at the CBI, said: "When we talk to members, the majority of them say the government has climate change firmly within its eyesight, and in that sense, national policy is a far larger driver."

However, the delay many now see as inevitable in sealing a global treaty was a serious concern.[British] Prime minister Gordon Brown said last night: "Every year of delay raises the cost of acting."

Professor Mohan Munasinghe, former vice-chair of the Intergovernmental Panel on Climate Change, said: "I doubt very much whether [a global deal] will happen in 2010, and it will likely be too late after that [to avoid dangerous global warming]."

For Tom Burke, the director of the environmental policy NGO [non-governmental organization] E3G, the delay will be unwelcome but instructive. "The accord is not going to go anywhere except in the headlines. It has no machinery and no resources outside of the UNFCCC, so everything will have to go back to the UNFCCC to get done. Think of the period between Bali [in 2007] and Copenhagen as the most expensive political education exercise in history. It is going to take some time to digest all the lessons but when we, collectively, have done so we will find that we are back pretty much to the start—but in a far worse climate."

Phil Bloomer, Oxfam's director of campaigns, was more blunt: "Every year we delay an estimated 150,000 people will have died and a further 1 million displaced as a result of climate change."

13

Enforcement of a Global Climate Agreement Would Be Difficult

Ravi Nessman and Rod McGuirk

Ravi Nessman and Rod McGuirk are international reporters for the Associated Press.

Implementation of a global climate treaty could be even more difficult than thus-far failed efforts to get one passed. Worldwide it is possible to point out many obstacles that would make meaningful enforcement of a climate treaty almost impossible.

For Indonesian farmers, burning down rain forests is the cheapest and fastest way to clear land for palm oil and pulp and paper plantations.

The millions of acres they burn every year has made their Southeast Asian nation the world's third-largest producer of greenhouse gases. And, environmentalists warn, the powerful forestry and agricultural industry will likely stymie any efforts to crack down.

As difficult as it may be to hammer out a global climate deal in Copenhagen [climate conference in December 2009], implementing one could prove even harder.

Obstacles to Change Are Great

From New Delhi to Washington, domestic political opposition, corruption, grass-roots intransigence and sheer bureaucratic incompetence stand as significant roadblocks to any agreement on emissions curbs.

Many across the globe are hoping Indonesia, with 10 percent of the worlds' forests, can be a leader in rain-forest preservation.

"But I think everybody has yet to realize how difficult this is going to be," said Frances Seymour, director-general of the Indonesia-based Center for International Forestry Research.

Using fire to clear land is illegal in Indonesia, but prosecutions are rare, said Greenpeace spokesman Brian Martin. Almost 18 million acres (7.2 million hectares) of land was burned during the last dry season from January to mid-October [2009], said Ali Akbar, an activist from the Indonesian Forum on Environment.

While reducing emissions has broad political support here, activists question whether the government has the political will to take on mismanagement and corruption in the regulation of the forestry industry, which costs the country an estimated $2 billion a year.

"It will take strong action at the top levels of Indonesian government and international trading partners to halt the corruption in the timber industry," Human Rights Watch deputy program director Joe Saunders said.

No Easy Solutions

The challenges are great across the world.

In the U.S., getting the treaty ratified, even by a Democrat-controlled Senate, will be a battle.

Republicans have charged that the emissions cuts President Barack Obama plans to offer at Copenhagen would cost jobs, making moderate Democrats nervous.

Some have urged Obama to be cautious about what he agrees to, knowing full well that the last time a U.S. administration signed an international climate treaty in the late 1990s in Kyoto, the Senate balked at ratifying it. The concern then—and now—was exceptions in the deal for developing countries, among the fastest-growing emitters of greenhouse gases.

Developing countries face their own dilemmas.

South Africa, facing severe domestic pressure to resolve energy shortages, is committed to building more coal-powered plants, angering activists.

"If (President Jacob) Zuma is in Copenhagen, he should have first cleaned his house," said Makoma Lekalakala, a South African environmentalist. "Renewable energy is an option and at the moment that is not exploited. The government needs to have political will to invest in renewable technologies."

Without Enforcement, Laws Make Little Difference

In India, failed efforts to clean up its rivers are instructive of how difficult it could be to clean up the air.

Despite a 2001 Supreme Court ruling ordering the cleanup of the Yamuna River, despite billions in government spending to do just that, the waterway that supplies 70 percent of New Delhi's water remains a frothy, putrid sewer.

"Twenty five years ago, I used to drink from here," said Om Prakash, a 72-year-old priest sitting near a canal dumping sewage into the river. "Nobody is taking care of Mother Yamuna."

A report from the New Delhi-based Center for Science and Environment blamed in part the improper placement of treatment plants, along with fights between water-starved states over managing the river water.

The corruption and bureaucracy that derails many public initiatives in India are factors too.

In the industrial town of Kanpur, along the Ganges, officials say factories are ignoring regulations and dumping untreated sewage and industrial pollution, turning the holy river into a toxic wasteland.

"Laws are there to prevent industries from pouring their waste into the Ganges, but we need their implementation in letter and spirit," said Alok Ranjan, a local urban development official.

Some Remain Hopeful

Still, many activists expressed optimism that India would have an easier time raising fuel efficiency standards for cars, reducing emissions from new power plants and establishing more efficient building codes than it had in trying to clean up the rivers.

India, which ranks fifth in the world in carbon dioxide emissions, pledged last week to slow the growth of its emissions significantly over the next decade.

"We are a country in a mess, but I think we have the financial, technical and technological means to climb out of this mess. And there is a sliver of hope that we will," said Bittu Sahgal, editor of Sanctuary Asia, an environmental magazine.

The country faces a host of hurdles: powerful state governments that often clash with the central government, a deeply entrenched bureaucracy and little history of conservation.

Sitting near the Yamuna's bank, Mohan Lal, 61, said he's seen personal attitudes to the environment changing and has himself grown more concerned about littering.

"Slowly and steadily, people are realizing these things have to be taken care of," he said. Then he took a long sip from his tea, swung his arm and threw the plastic cup into the brush.

14

Governments Worldwide Must Work Together to Reduce Carbon Emissions

Sir John Houghton

Sir John Houghton, formerly a professor of atmospheric physics at Oxford University, is the co-chairman of the International Panel on Climate Change Scientific Assessment Working Group.

Despite the disappointing outcome of the world climate change conference in Copenhagen in late 2009, some important outcomes were identified in the conference's final document, the Copenhagen Accord. The urgent challenge now is to restore momentum. Working either individually or multilaterally, governments must create a long term policy framework that can induce business and industry to move forward with investments in carbon-free energy projects.

> *When written in Chinese the word crisis is composed of two characters, one represents danger and the other represents opportunity.*
>
> *President John F. Kennedy*

A t the world climate change conference in Copenhagen from the 7th to the 18th December 2009, tens of thousand of delegates, representatives of NGOs [non-governmental organizations] and other interested parties gathered with great

Sir John Houghton, "Copenhagen and the Climate Change Crisis," *The JRI Briefing Papers—No. 19*, February 16, 2010. Reproduced by permission.

expectation. What was hoped for was an outcome binding the world's governments to halt damaging human-induced climate change. But no such agreements were forthcoming. Nor was there agreement over a timetable to make such agreements. All very disappointing. So what, if anything, was achieved and what needs to be done now to bring the process back on track?

The final document of the conference called the *Copenhagen Accord* was brokered by the United States, China, India, South Africa and Brazil and just noted by the conference (188 nations in all). It included some important positive outcomes namely:

1. A near-global consensus for a goal of 2°C [Celsius] for the maximum rise of global average temperature from its preindustrial value due to human activities—a tough but necessary target.

2. Developed countries committed to implementing quantified economy-wide emissions targets for 2020 at levels to be notified by the 31 January 2010.

3. Developing countries will register mitigation actions that are self-supported. Actions by developing countries that receive support from other nations will be monitored by an international inspection regime.

4. Funding to be provided by developed countries to developing countries to assist in their adaptation to climate change and their mitigation actions. No definite or binding agreements were made and doubts were expressed whether the funding would be new and additional to existing countries' funding commitments. However an aim was declared to raise about 30 billion US dollars for the years 2010–2012 and about 100 billion US dollars per year by 2020 from a wide variety of sources.

5. An assessment of implementation is to be made by 2015 including the possible need to strengthen the long term goal by changing the maximum temperature rise to 1.5°C.

The consensus in (1) above is of fundamental importance. That it has emerged intact from the conference demonstrates a high level of concern throughout the world about the damaging impacts of climate change and a general recognition that strong action needs to be taken.

For (2) above it is essential that Developed Countries offer not just token reductions by 2020, but substantial and meaningful reductions. The offer from the European Union is especially important. So far it is for a 20/30% reduction—30% if reductions by other nations are deemed adequate. However, if it could be for 40% reduction as has already been agreed in Wales and Scotland, it would provide a serious lead for other developed nations to follow.

The agreement about international inspection in (3) above was vital for President Obama to take away from the conference. Without it, there would be real difficulty for the bill regarding reductions of greenhouse gases in the USA to be passed by the US Senate next Spring.

After such a disappointing outcome in Copenhagen that began with a great sense of importance and urgency, the problem will be to get back on track.

The funding mentioned in (4) above, which is still only an aim, is important as it indicates that developed countries recognise at least some responsibility (although as I explain below, nothing like enough) for the plight of developing countries many of which will suffer serious damage as climate change begins to bite.

The assessment in 2015, 5 years away, mentioned in (5) above can only provide a 'long stop' for the process. It is essential that within one year—by the time of the next Conference of Parties of the Climate Convention (COP16) to be held in Mexico late in 2010—commitments and agreements are made by the world's countries adequate to meet the goal of 2°C set out in (1) above. Indications so far (February 2010) from nations, developed and developing, about their likely commitments as mentioned in (2) above are more in line with a 3 or 4°C global average temperature goal rather than a 2°C goal. It is vital therefore that they be substantially strengthened during this year 2010.

The mention of a 1.5°C goal eventually being necessary perhaps demonstrates the beginning of a realization that the demands presented by anthropogenic climate change are likely to become much tougher in the future.

A further positive point about the conference that can be made is that no compromise agreements, for instance regarding reductions of emissions to inadequate levels, were made at Copenhagen. Better to have no agreement rather than one that is clearly unsatisfactory.

What Is Needed Now?

After such a disappointing outcome in Copenhagen that began with a great sense of importance and urgency, the problem will be to get back on track. Valuable time has been lost not least in providing the world's business and industrial sector with the policy certainty necessary to generate investments in energy and other technologies on the scale required to meet the 2°C goal. The sense of urgency, now even more necessary than before, is in danger of being lost in the post Copenhagen confusion.

Previous major meetings of the parties to the Climate Convention, such as in 1992 at the Earth Summit in Rio de Janeiro and when the Kyoto Protocol was agreed in 1997, have concluded with unanimous agreements from all the participating nations. However, some of those agreements failed to materialize in practice (for instance, the withdrawal of the USA from the Kyoto protocol) and it is probably unrealistic now to expect all the world's nations to come to unanimous agreement on such a complex issue—at least without a great deal of preliminary work being done by different national groupings. Hopefully the experiences of Copenhagen will spark initiatives of the right kind.

There is a strong moral imperative for rich developed countries to recognise . . . that the main source of their wealth has been cheap energy provided by fossil fuels.

Preparations for the Mexico conference in 2010 must be much more thorough and detailed than those for Copenhagen and need to include serious bilateral and multilateral discussions. That such discussions can be effective is illustrated by the largely political statement called the *accord* that came out of the Copenhagen meeting and that resulted from hastily arranged discussions between the leaders of some of the nations that contribute most to carbon emissions. Of greatest importance are bilateral agreements that the US and China might be able to achieve—between them they account for nearly half the world's emissions. The G20 [group of 20 finance ministers and central bank governers] should also be seriously involved. If during the next year groupings of nations could work together on a time table of joint action to achieve the 2°C target, the Mexico conference later this year might be able to draw all nations into the more complete arrangement that is required.

Developing Nations Are Not Satisfied

At the start of the Copenhagen meeting, strong appeals and demands were made by developing nations to developed nations for a recognition that, since emissions from developed nations had largely caused the damage so far, these nations had an obligation to assist developing countries towards their adaptation to climate change and their mitigation actions. Although some progress on this issue was eventually made—though lacking definite agreement as to how much developed countries would eventually provide—developing nations were far from satisfied with these discussions across the rich/poor divide.

There is a strong moral imperative for rich developed countries to recognise (1) that the main source of their wealth has been cheap energy provided by fossil fuels, (2) that substantial damage is occurring because of the resulting climate change, disproportionately to poorer countries, and (3) that they should reduce their own emissions as rapidly as possible and show willingness to provide generous assistance with wealth and skills to enable poorer countries to adapt to climate change and to develop in sustainable ways. Christians who follow Jesus in his great concern for caring for the poor should be in the forefront in pressing this imperative. . . .

Sustainable Development Is a Moral Imperative

I have presented some reflections on the outcome of the Copenhagen Conference and have expressed the danger that with reduced momentum in the negotiation process and the absence of any agreed timetable for getting back on track, the fierce urgency of the need for action *now* could be lost.

A window of opportunity exists during this year of 2010 for action to be taken to secure a future that avoids very serious future climate changes that are most likely irreversible. It is encouraging that industries and investors in many countries are keen to grow carbon-free energy projects. But urgent action by governments (acting singly, bilaterally or multilaterally) is needed to create an effective, imaginative long term policy framework that will provide confidence to business and industry to move forward, in partnership with governments as necessary, with a rapid and effective investment programme to reduce global greenhouse gas emissions. To achieve the goal of 2°C maximum global temperature increase, future global emissions must peak well before 2020, then fall as rapidly as possible to below 50% of 1990 levels before 2050 and close to zero well before the end of the century.

A further essential aim must be for a successful outcome to COP16 [the sixteenth Conference of Parties under the United Nations Framework Convention on Climate Change] in Mexico in December 2010.

I have pointed out the very strong moral imperative that applies to the developed world to share their wealth and skills with the developing world as they adapt to damaging climate change and seek to develop sustainably. I have also argued that, for the strong necessary action by governments, business and industry to be possible, it is important for the basic facts of the science and consequences of climate change to be better understood and accepted by the population at large. Urgent consideration needs to be given to the practical measures required for this to be achieved. It presents an enormous challenge to all of us and to many organisations. I believe that grasping the challenge is particularly urgent for Christians and other faith communities whose combined action could make a large difference.

15

Development of Clean Energy Should Be the Focus of Climate Policy

The Economist

The Economist is a weekly international news and business publication.

Recent international efforts to address climate change have not been successful. According to the authors of the Hartwell paper, a report on climate change policy by a group of academics and activists in the United Kingdom, these efforts have failed because their architects have not understood that climate change is "a persistent condition that must be coped with and can only be partially managed more—or less—well." Instead of climate change and reducing carbon emissions, the focus should instead be on creating a world with accessible clean and secure low-cost energy for all.

What does climate policy have to learn from Capability Brown, whose landscape designs provided the settings for over a hundred of England's stately homes and palaces in the 18th century? According to a new discussion paper by a group of academics and policy activists, the answer is a form of stage management. Brown eschewed long straight drives that took the visitor directly from the edge of a property to the house at its heart, feeling the destination was diminished and made dull by being always straight ahead. He preferred that people travel along winding "lines of grace" and "lines of beauty", in the aesthetic idiom of the time. He arranged the curves and contours of the landscape, with its woods and glades and lakes, in such a way as to frame and then hide the object of the journey in various delightful ways before the final, impressive arrival. "Lose the object and draw nigh obliquely," he is said to have said.

A Beeline to the Goal Hasn't Worked

This is the lesson that a number of academics, mostly from the social sciences and humanities, and other interested parties, drew from a meeting they held in February [2010] to discuss the perceived failures of the approach to climate change that the world has been following for the past two decades. (They were helped by the fact that their meeting place, Hartwell House near Aylesbury, benefits from fine grounds landscaped in Brown's style.) Taking the climate itself as the object of policy, and making a beeline for a climate endpoint that you have been told is desirable—a world less than two degrees warmer than the one Brown enjoyed in the 18th century is the widely accepted target—is an approach which has failed to have much practical impact to date. In a discussion paper drafted since the meeting and released on May 11th, the Hartwell group argues that that lack of impact is unavoidable. Slogging doggedly to a distant end that seems never to get any closer is not going to work: to make progress one needs to follow a more roundabout route, one which is a pleasure—or at least politically appealing—at every point on the journey.

The difficulty with the current approach to climate change, according to the Hartwell paper, is that climate change is not a problem. A problem can be identified, isolated and, in principle, solved. Climate change isn't like that: it is "better understood as a persistent condition that must be coped with and can only be partially managed more—or less—well." This is not a new point. Various Hartwellites, and others, have been making it for some time. Steve Rayner of Oxford and Gwyn Prins of the LSE [London School of Economics], who were in effect the conveners of the Hartwell meeting, did so in a 2007 paper called "The Wrong Trousers", evoking the out-of-control robot clothing that takes its inventor to places he would rather not go in the animated movie of the same name. (The Hartwellite school of analysis is not without a strain of high-table whimsy some will find off-putting.)

Last year these ideas were worked through by Mike Hulme, a professor at the University of East Anglia and another Hartwellite, in his thought provoking book *Why We Disagree about Climate Change*. The reason, Hulme argued, was not that some people are inadequately informed, as is often assumed, but because different people see the issue from different perspectives and in different contexts.

Following a path stressing clean energy as a development issue provides a more pleasant journey to the same objective.

Searching for a More Compelling Strategy

The consensus view of climate change rejects this messy plurality by framing the issue as a classical environmental problem—in effect, carbon-dioxide pollution—and looking for a solution in the form of policies that directly or indirectly reduce the amount or carbon dioxide people emit. Climate diplomacy tries, at its best, to provide a range of strategies by which different countries with different capabilities can cooperate towards this common end, on the basis that natural science has revealed it to be what everyone wants, or should want. The degree to which debates about climate change have become debates about climate-change science reflects the fact that this way of looking at the issue presents "the science" as a reason to act; those who want action thus have an interest in exaggerrating the conclusions or certainty of the science, and those who do not wish to act are incentivised in the opposite direction.

The Hartwellites do not disagree with the science in general and certainly don't think there is no reason to act. They simply doubt that action along this one axis (carbon-dioxide reduction) can ever be made politically compelling. Instead, their oblique strategies . . . are to concentrate on easy opportunities and efficiency, energy and dignity.

The easy opportunities that they highlight include getting rid of a lot of black carbon (atmospheric soot) and ozone in the lower atmosphere; both are responsible for a lot of harm independent of the warming that they cause, and thus easier to act against than carbon dioxide. Others have made this point, but it doesn't hurt to repeat it, since it is a good one. They approve of reducing deforestation, too, which is a completely mainstream view. A stress on making sure that the capacity to adapt to climate change is treated as seriously as the need to avoid it in the first place, rather than as some sort of admission of defeat, is less mainstream, but it is still within the current political consensus.

Where the Hartwell paper becomes controversial is in its approach to decarbonisation. The authors argue that the large emerging economies are clearly fuelling themselves with renewables and nuclear as well as, rather than instead of, fossil fuels, for various reasons, and that this will not change soon. Nor, they imply, should it. They argue that there is something wrong with a world in which carbon-dioxide levels are kept to 450 parts per million (a trajectory widely deemed compatible with a 2 degree cap on warming) but at the same time more than a billion of the poorest people are left without electricity, as in one much discussed scenario from the International Energy Agency.

Their oblique approach is to aim instead for a world with accessible, secure low cost energy for all. The hope, intuition or strategy at play here is that since fossil fuels cannot deliver such a world, its achievement will, in itself, bring about decarbonisation on a massive scale. Following a path stressing clean energy as a development issue provides a more pleasant journey to the same objective.

While reframing the climate issue around energy and equity is undoubtedly appealing, it is not clear how effective it would be as a policy.

Looking for Energy that Really Is Cheap

This analysis moves the policy prescription away from making today's fossil fuels more expensive while subsidising the use of current suboptimal renewables, and towards the development of new energy technologies that will be cheap in absolute terms. This is to be achieved by spending public money directly on the development of the new technologies needed, rather than by hoping that putting a price on carbon will naturally move the market to the same destination. When it comes to technology development, the message is a distinctly un-Brownian "go straight for what you want" that will be familiar to those who have come across California think tank The Breakthrough Institute, the founders of which were also among the authors of the Hartwell paper.

There is much to like in the Hartwell analysis, but also a lot to question. While reframing the climate issue around energy and equity is undoubtedly appealing, it is not clear how effective it would be as a policy. One of the reasons so much interaction and conflict between rich and poor countries now goes on within the context of climate change negotiations is that those negotiations provide the developing countries with some leverage, both moral and institutional. To go from that situation to something more like the *a la carte* approach or the [United Nations'] Millennium Development Goals or the commitments to Africa made at Gleneagles [summit in 2005 in Scotland] would not necessarily be progress.

Another problem is that people have a great deal invested in the established world view; it will not be dismantled and reassembled easily. Brown's pleasingly oblique approaches required back-breaking and carefully orchestrated work with shovels and wheelbarrows, not to mention the removal or flooding of the occasional insufficiently picturesque hamlet. On the question of the analagous work required to bring about the change of perspectives it imagines, the Hartwell paper is rather silent.

And then there is the question of time. Though the paper is not explicit on this, to accept that decarbonisation will require as-yet unavailable technologies to achieve deep penetration around the world is to accept that carbon-dioxide levels will get a lot higher than current policies want them to. Which might seem a good enough reason to reject the whole idea. Except that the current policies have not, as yet, made a very great deal of difference. The straight road seems to be one travelled slowly, even if it looks shorter.

Organizations to Contact

The editors have compiled the following list of organizations concerned with the issues debated in this book. The descriptions are derived from materials provided by the organizations. All have publications or information available for interested readers. The list was compiled on the date of publication of the present volume; street and online addresses may change. Be aware that many organizations take several weeks or longer to respond to inquiries, so allow as much time as possible.

American Enterprise Institute for Public Policy Research (AEI)
1150 Seventeenth St. NW, Washington, DC   20036
(202) 862-5800
website: www.aei.org

AEI scholars support the organization's values of private liberty, individual opportunity, and free enterprise by emphasizing the need to design policies that protect nature while fostering economic growth and productivity. One of the institute's eight major research areas is the topic of energy and the environment, which encompasses environmental policy and regulation, energy policy and climate change. The AEI website contains articles, speeches, testimony, and other published materials that address climate change, economics, and regulatory issues.

Center for American Progress Action Fund
1333 H St. NW, 10th Floor, Washington, DC   20005
(202) 682-1611
website: www.americanprogressaction.org

The Center for American Progress (CAP) Action Fund is a progressive think tank that works to transform progressive ideas into policy through legislative action, grassroots organizing, and advocacy. The Climate Progress blog, a publication of CAP, advocates for a progressive perspective on climate science, climate solutions, and climate politics. *Time Magazine* named Climate Progress one of the "Best Blogs of 2010."

Ceres
99 Chauncy St., 6th Floor, Boston, MA   02111
(617) 247-0700
website: www.ceres.org

Ceres is a coalition of investors and environmentalists concerned about the development of sustainable prosperity. The Ceres website archives business news as well as its own reports on climate change and other environmental issues, economic policy, and sustainable development.

Heartland Institute
19 S LaSalle St., Suite 903, Chicago, IL   60603
(312) 377-4000
website: www.heartland.org

The Heartland Institute is a nonprofit research and education organization. Heartland's mission is to discover, develop, and promote free-market solutions to social and economic problems, including environmental protection. The Center for Climate and Environmental Policy at the Heartland Institute publishes *Environment & Climate News*, which is accessible from the organization's website.

The Heritage Foundation
214 Massachusetts Ave. NE, Washington, DC   20002-4999
(202) 546-4400
website: www.heritage.org

The Heritage Foundation is a research and educational institution. Its mission is to formulate and promote conservative public policies based on the principles of free enterprise, limited government, individual freedom, traditional American values, and a strong national defense. The Heritage Foundation website includes a section devoted to energy and the environment.

Intergovernmental Panel on Climate Change (IPCC)
c/o World Meteorological Organization
7bis Avenue de la Paix, C.P. 2300
Geneva 2   CH-1211
  Switzerland
website: www.ipcc.ch

The Intergovernmental Panel on Climate Change is a scientific body that was established by the United Nations. It reviews and assesses the most recent scientific, technical, and socioeconomic information relevant to the understanding of climate change. The mission of the IPCC is to provide reliable and authoritative scientific information to governmental decisionmakers. The IPCC website archives the organization's reports, speeches, presentations and other publications.

International Energy Agency (IEA)
9, Rue de la Fédération, Paris   75015
  France
website: www.iea.org/index.asp

Starting in the 1970s, the International Energy Agency's role was to coordinate an international response to oil supply emergencies. Its current work focuses on climate change policies, market reform, and energy technology collaboration. IEA publishes reports—*World Energy Outlook* and *Energy Technology Perspectives*—that are posted on the IEA website.

Natural Resources Defense Council (NRDC)
40 W 20th St., New York, NY   10011
(212) 727-2700
website: www.nrdc.org

The Natural Resources Defense Council is an environmental action organization that works to protect wildlife and wild places and to ensure a safe and healthy environment for all living things. The NRDC website tags articles and reports on the topic of global warming legislation.

Pew Center on Global Climate Change

2101 Wilson Blvd., Suite 550, Arlington, VA   22201
(703) 516-4146
website: www.pewclimate.org

The Pew Center on Global Climate Change conducts analysis and organizes information on key climate issues and engages the business community in the search for solutions. The center's website includes sections on global warming, science and impacts, and technology solutions. It also hosts a page with up-to-date information on international climate negotiations and a feature that enables users to calculate their personal carbon footprints.

Physicians for Social Responsibility (PSR)

1875 Connecticut Ave. NW, Suite 1012
Washington, DC   20009
(202) 667-4260
website: www.psr.org

Physicians for Social Responsibility is a nonprofit advocacy organization whose membership includes health professionals and other concerned citizens. Established to educate the public about the health dangers of nuclear proliferation, PSR recently launched a campaign to support climate and energy legislation. The PSR website publishes information about environmental toxins and global warming as issues affecting public health.

Union of Concerned Scientists (UCS)

Two Brattle Square, Cambridge, MA   02138-3780
(617) 547-5552
website: www.ucsusa.org

The Union of Concerned Scientists is a science-based nonprofit that works for a healthy environment and a safer world. It conducts independent scientific research and supports citizen action to develop solutions and to secure changes in government policy, corporate practices, and consumer choices. The UCS website includes information on the science of global warming and the status of regional efforts to address climate change.

United Nations Development Programme (UNDP)
304 E 45th St., 9th Floor, New York, NY   10017
e-mail: minoru.takada@undp.org
website: www.undp.org

The United Nations Development Programme supports developing countries in responding to climate change concerns as part of their overall sustainable development efforts. Its primary focus is to improve the lives of those living in extreme poverty. The UNDP website includes information about the impact of climate change on developing countries, and on programs to support clean energy technology in the developing world.

US Environmental Protection Agency (EPA)
Ariel Rios Bldg., 1200 Pennsylvania Ave. NW
Washington, DC   20460
(202) 272-0167
website: www.epa.gov

The Environmental Protection Agency's climate change programs and activities are part of its mission to protect human health and the environment. The EPA climate change page on its website includes sections explaining the current science of climate change and US climate policy.

USAID Global Climate Change Program
Ronald Reagan Bldg., Washington, DC   20523-1000
(202) 712-4810
website: www.usaid.gov

USAID is the US Agency for International Development and efforts to address the causes and effects of climate change is a key focus of USAID's development assistance program. US-

AID enters into partnerships with the private sector and works with local and national authorities, communities, and nongovernmental organizations to reduce carbon dioxide emissions. The website provides information on USAID's Global Climate Change Program and posts current articles and reports on climate science, clean energy technology, sustainable land use, and United States participation in the United Nations Framework Convention on Climate Change.

Bibliography

Books

Joseph E. Aldy
and R.N. Stavins
Architectures for Agreement: Addressing Global Climate Change in the Post-Kyoto World. New York: Cambridge University Press, 2007.

Stephen F.
Bernstein
A Globally Integrated Climate Policy for Canada. Toronto: University of Toronto Press, 2008.

Patricia W. Birnie,
Alan E. Boyle,
and Catherine
Redgwell
International Law and the Environment. New York: Oxford University Press, 2009.

Lael Brainard,
Abigail Jones, and
Nigel Purvis
Climate Change and Global Poverty: A Billion Lives in the Balance? Washington, DC: Brookings Institution Press, 2009.

Andrew Dessler
and Edward A.
Parson
The Science and Politics of Global Climate Change: A Guide to the Debate. New York: Cambridge University Press, 2010.

Kirsten Dow and
Thomas E.
Downing
The Atlas of Climate Change: Mapping the World's Greatest Challenge. Berkeley, CA: University of California Press, 2006.

Tim F. Flannery   *Now or Never: Why We Must Act Now to End Climate Change and Create a Sustainable Future.* New York: Atlantic Monthly Press, 2009.

Al Gore   *An Inconvenient Truth: The Crisis of Global Warming.* New York: Viking, 2007.

Mayer Hillman, Tina Fawcett, and Sudhir Chella Rajan   *The Suicidal Planet: How to Prevent Global Climate Catastrophe.* New York: Thomas Dunne Books/St. Martin's Press, 2007.

Bjorn Lomborg   *Smart Solutions to Climate Change: Comparing Costs and Benefits.* New York: Cambridge University Press, 2010.

Eric Pooley   *The Climate War: True Believers, Power Brokers, and the Fight to Save the Earth.* New York: Hyperion, 2010.

Eric A. Posner and David A. Weisbach   *Climate Change Justice.* Princeton, NJ: Princeton University Press, 2010.

Joseph J. Romm   *Hell and High Water: Global Warming—The Solution and the Politics—and What We Should Do.* New York: William Morrow, 2007.

Stephen Henry Schneider   *Science as a Contact Sport: Inside the Battle to Save Earth's Climate.* Washington, DC: National Geographic, 2009.

S. Fred Singer and Dennis T. Avery — *Unstoppable Global Warming: Every 1500 Years.* Lanham, MD: Rowman & Littlefield Publishers, 2007.

James Gustave Speth and Peter M. Hass — *Global Environmental Governance.* Washington, DC: Island Press, 2006.

N.H. Stern — *The Global Deal: Climate Change and the Creation of a New Era of Progress and Prosperity.* New York: PublicAffairs, 2009.

Michael Tennesen — *The Complete Idiot's Guide to Global Warming.* New York: Alpha, 2008.

Gabrielle Walker and D.A. King — *The Hot Topic: What We Can Do About Global Warming.* Orlando, FL: Harcourt, 2008.

Periodicals

John M. Broder — "As Time Runs Short for Global Climate Treaty, Nations May Settle for Interim Steps," *New York Times*, October 20, 2009.

The Canadian Press — "Canada Signing Climate Treaty Without U.S. Like 'Unilateral Disarmament': Baird," *CBC News*, December 9, 2007.

Kim Chipman — "Climate Treaty Must Set Tough Emissions Limits, Scientists Say," *Bloomberg*, December 6, 2007.

David Di Martino   "Another Poll Shows Narrative on Climate Change Is Dead Wrong," *The Hill*, October 27, 2010.

Earth Times   "ANALYSIS: Obama Flat, China Mixed, Japan Wins at UN Climate Summit," September 23, 2009.

Juliet Eilperin   "Climate Treaty Realities Push Leaders to Trim Priority Lists," *Washington Post*, April 13, 2010.

Environment News Service   "British Parliamentary Inquiry Clears 'Climategate' Scientists," March 31, 2010.

Lisa Friedman   "Wary Nations Face Cultural Divide on Climate Treaty's 'Transparency,'" *New York Times*, December 16, 2009.

Kent Garber   "'Reasonable' Progress on Climate Change Talks but Long Road Ahead, Says U.N. Official," *U.S. News and World Report*, December 15, 2008.

Julian Hunt   "Act Locally While Awaiting Global Climate Treaty," *The Australian*, October 8, 2010.

Irish Times   "Pope Condemns Climate Deal Failure," October 25, 2010.

Mark Lynas   "How Do I Know China Wrecked the Copenhagen Deal? I Was in the Room," *The Guardian*, December 22, 2009.

Michael McCarthy	"Britain Rules Out Climate Treaty at Summit," *The Independent*, November 6, 2009.
Jan M. Olsen	"Deadlock Between Rich, Poor Countries Makes Climate Deal Unlikely, Danish Official Says," *Cleveland Plain Dealer*, December 17, 2009.
Mackubin Thomas Owens	"EPA Global Warmers' Power Grab," *Washington Times*, October 11, 2010.
Susan Page	"Most Back a Treaty on Global Warming," *USA Today*, December 15, 2009.
Fred Pearce	"Is It Time to Say Goodbye Cool World?" *New Scientist*, June 15, 2010.
Andrew Restuccia	"Where Does the Country Stand on Climate Change," *The Washington Independent*, October 28, 2010.
Andrew C. Revkin	"On Balance, Hype, Climate and the Media," *New York Times*, October 26, 2010.
Elizabeth Rosenthal	"UN Talks Set Nations on Path to Global Climate Treaty," *Boston Globe*, December 13, 2008.
Darren Samuelsohn	"No 'Pass' for Developing Countries in Next Climate Treaty, Says U.S. Envoy," *New York Times*, December 9, 2009.

Gregor Peter Schmitz — "U.S. Stance on Climate Change: Yes We Can—But Not Yet," *Spiegel,* September 22, 2009.

Mark Scott — "Copenhagen: Business Wants Clarity," *Businessweek,* December 14, 2009.

Peter N. Spotts — "A Global Warming Summit of Good Intentions," *Christian Science Monitor,* September 23, 2009.

Peter N. Spotts — "Copenhagen Climate Change Talks Stall as Emissions Rise," *Christian Science Monitor,* November 18, 2009.

Jim Tankersley — "Businesspeople Join the Ranks of Climate Treaty Proponents," *Los Angeles Times,* December 12, 2009.

The Times of India — "Climate Change Treaty Must Address Health Issues: WHO," October 19, 2010.

US Senate, Committee on Foreign Relations — *International Climate Change Negotiations: Bali and the Path Toward a Post-2012 Climate Treaty—Hearing before the Committee on Foreign Relations,* January 24, 2008.

Wall Street Journal — "The Tip of the Climategate Iceberg: The Global-Warming Scandal Is Bigger Than One Email Leak," December 8, 2009.

Index